T0318216

Teaching Through Embodied Learning

Teaching Through Embodied Learning positions drama as an under-utilised but valuable tool for enhancing the learning of information in primary science texts. Creating a 'tableau' is an established drama practice for exploring key moments in fiction texts and historical events but less frequently applied with non-fiction texts. Based on doctoral research that studied the impact of having students create a tableau in response to reading informational texts about the solar system, it presents the idea that using drama with informational texts causes students to read purposefully and respond aesthetically; thus, positively impacting reading behaviour, comprehension and social behaviour.

The book addresses the neglect of the body in learning and positions this against a narrow curriculum that is focused on print and 'seated learning'. Within a current context, it acknowledges increasing concerns by educational leaders and academics of the need for a 'broad and balanced curriculum' and pedagogical practice. In support of these concerns, the book places tableau as an embodied learning mode that broadens curriculum experience and discusses recent research that highlights the role of drama and the body in enhancing cognition.

Teaching Through Embodied Learning will be essential reading for academics, researchers and post-graduate students in the fields of education and drama education. It will also greatly appeal to teacher educators, drama teachers and academics in literacy departments.

Margaret V. Branscombe is an experienced teacher and has applied drama across the curriculum in primary, secondary and Higher Education contexts. She has a PhD in Literacy Studies from the University of South Florida. She is a Literacy Intervention teacher and her website can be found at www. learnthroughdrama.com.

Teaching Through Embodied Learning

Dramatizing Key Concepts from Informational Texts

Margaret V. Branscombe

Routledge
Taylor & Francis Group

LONDON AND NEW YORK

First published 2019
by Routledge

2 Park Square, Milton Park, Abingdon, Oxfordshire OX14 4RN
52 Vanderbilt Avenue, New York, NY 10017

Routledge is an imprint of the Taylor & Francis Group, an informa business

First issued in paperback 2020

British Library Cataloguing-in-Publication Data
A catalogue record for this book is available from the British Library

Library of Congress Cataloging-in-Publication Data
Names: Branscombe, Margaret V., author.
Title: Teaching through embodied learning : dramatizing key concepts from
informational texts / Margaret V. Branscombe.
Description: Abingdon, Oxon ; New York, NY : Routledge, 2019. | Includes
bibliographical references.
Identifiers: LCCN 2018060185 (print) | LCCN 2019004611 (ebook) |
ISBN 9780429462986 (eBook) | ISBN 9781138615717 (hardback)
Subjects: LCSH: Science—Study and teaching (Primary) | Drama in
education. | Teaching—Aids and devices.
Classification: LCC LB1532 (ebook) | LCC LB1532 .B75 2019 (print) |
DDC 372.35/044—dc23
LC record available at https://lccn.loc.gov/2018060185

ISBN: 978-1-138-61571-7 (hbk)
ISBN: 978-0-367-67182-2 (pbk)

Typeset in Times New Roman
by Deanta Global Publishing Services, Chennai, India

I dedicate this book in memory of Jan Taylor, inspirational Head Teacher who taught me so much

Contents

Figures

Tables

Preface

In 2014, I conducted research for my PhD thesis in a third grade (Year 4) classroom in Florida, USA. As a former primary school teacher and literacy lead based in England, I had found drama to be a very effective medium for teaching a range of subjects. When I undertook my PhD in Literacy Studies at the University of South Florida, I focused my research on drama as a powerful tool for strengthening comprehension across the curriculum and my particular focus became using the body to represent scientific concepts.

The timing of my PhD coincided with a very 'interesting' period in American education. In 2010, the Common Core State Standards Initiative (CCSSI) was rolled out across the country in an attempt to introduce nationwide expectations in English and mathematics that would ensure all students were 'college and career ready' (National Governors Association Center for Best Practices, Council of Chief State School Officers, 2010). The CCSSI was contentious for many reasons and its implementation was rejected by some states on political and ideological grounds. The 'reading standards' made clear the need for greater text complexity in both fiction and information texts and attracted controversy because of a statement that asserted students should "read closely to determine what the text says explicitly and to make logical inferences from it". This was viewed by some as a rejection of what had been happening in many American classrooms where children were encouraged to bring their background knowledge and personal interpretations to reach an understanding of a text. I explain 'close reading' more thoroughly in Chapter 1, but the point is that as a literacy teacher I anticipated a future of increasingly restrictive reading practices. At the same time as the Common Core State Standards were published, public schools (state schools) were reporting a sharp decline in arts provision. Education cuts, high stakes testing and teacher accountability had resulted in a curriculum devoid of innovative approaches to learning and fewer chances for children to learn about and through the expressive arts particularly (see Table P.1).

It felt like a perfect storm for conditions that could make my research interest in drama simultaneously challenging and yet more relevant than ever.

In the light of what was happening, I realised the need to design a study permissible in a Common Core context that placed drama outside the remit of literacy teaching. Working within this constraint but determined to integrate drama, I designed a study that required elementary (Key Stage 2) students to read science information texts 'closely' as a prelude for the dramatic representation of main ideas. My research plan was not purely strategic though. I believed bringing science and drama together would make for a fascinating study and contribute to the movement advocating for a STEAM curriculum (science, technology, engineering, arts and mathematics).

My proposal to conduct the research in a local school did not go according to plan. The first school district (local authority) I approached rejected my application for classroom research on the grounds that it would take too much time away from regular classroom instruction. An application to another school district was also rejected because the district did not allow research that generated new data. The rejections started to tell a story that was interesting in itself and I have written about this more fully elsewhere (Anderson, Branscombe & Nkrumah, 2015). Given the rejections by two large school districts, I had no option but to approach a charter school. Charter schools, like academies in the United Kingdom, receive state funding but can operate independently of local authority control. The charter school I approached was very positive about my research agenda and I was able to implement the classroom study that became the impetus for this book.

Table P.1 Percentages of public elementary schools reporting instruction in the arts for 1999–2000 and 2009–2010, USA

Art instruction	1999–2000	2009–2010
Music	94%	94%
Visual arts	87%	83%
Dance	20%	3%
Drama	20%	4%

Note. See Parsad & Spiegelman (2012), p. 5.

I acknowledge the information above is a personal account but I believe it gives an important context for how this book came to be written. The fact that my research, and the accompanying struggles to conduct the research, happened in the United States does not matter. Sadly, here in the United Kingdom I am experiencing a curriculum and ideology that is squeezing out opportunities for expressive practices and engaging the whole body in learning. But it doesn't have to be like this. As a practising teacher and researcher I have witnessed the significant benefits that drama can bring to learning. Which is why I wrote the book – to further the cause of embodied teaching practices that make learning more varied, interesting and memorable.

As a final note, the irony of writing a book calling for the dismantling of a logocentric curriculum and a greater emphasis on the body is not lost on me! It is my hope, however, that the words of this book will inspire readers to, quite literally, *move* beyond the print and incorporate the body in their teaching and learning. After all, as Boal reminds us: "The human being, first and foremost, is a body" (1995, p. 29).

References

Anderson, A.W., Branscombe, M., & Nkrumah, T. (2015). Blocked thresholds: Three stories of identity, embodied literacy, and participatory education. *Journal of Language and Literacy Education*, [Online] 11(2).

Boal, A. (1995). *The rainbow of desire*. London, United Kingdom: Routledge.

National Governors Association Center for Best Practices, Council of Chief State School Officers. (2010). *Common core state standards*. National Governors Association Center for Best Practices, Council of Chief State School Officers, Washington, DC.

Parsad, B., & Spiegelman, M. (2012). *Arts education in public elementary and secondary schools: 1999–2000 and 2009–10* (NCES 2012–014). National Center for Education Statistics, Institute of Education Sciences, U.S. Department of Education. Washington, DC. Retrieved from http://nces.ed.gov/pubs 2012/2012014rev.pdf

Acknowledgements

My thanks go to Dr Jenifer Jasinski Schneider, Professor of Literacy Studies at the University of South Florida. Thank you for encouraging me to share this research and believing in its importance. Also, many thanks to Mike, Ella and Grace. I couldn't have done this without your love and support. Keep on moving!

1 And then we focus on their heads

Setting the scene

More than a decade has passed since Sir Ken Robinson delivered his TED talk, "Do Schools Kill Creativity?" and yet it remains the most watched talk to date. When shared with groups of teachers in training, I have observed how the content of this talk unfailingly touches a pedagogical nerve of significance as he dissects the institutional and historical ways in which schools have dulled the creative potential of their students. Robinson, presumably along with many of those who have watched and shared the talk more than once, believes that many schools are indeed guilty of killing creativity, and a central thesis of his argument rests with the hierarchical structure of the curriculum schools deliver:

> At the top are mathematics and languages, then the humanities, and at the bottom are the arts. Everywhere on Earth. And in pretty much every system too, there's a hierarchy within the arts. Art and music are normally given a higher status in schools than drama and dance. There isn't an education system on the planet that teaches dance everyday to children the way we teach them mathematics. I think maths is very important, but so is dance. Children dance all the time if they're allowed to, we all do. We all have bodies, don't we?
>
> (Robinson, 2006, 8:28)

Robinson's rhetorical question here is followed by this critique, "Truthfully, what happens is, as children grow up, we start to educate them progressively from the waist up. And then we focus on their heads". The 'focus on their heads' description of education in 2006 has become an even more fitting indictment in 2018, and I believe the seemingly obvious recognition that we do all have bodies is needed now more than ever. In the United Kingdom presently, secondary schools are reporting declining numbers of students enrolling for programmes of study that give particular focus to the use of the body, i.e. dance and drama (Adams, 2017; Turner, 2017). Geoff Barton, former Head Teacher and general secretary of the Association of School and College Leaders, has been a vocal critic of Government measures which he believes have resulted in students not selecting arts subjects for study at Key Stage 4 (2017). Barton advocates for the arts as a "birthright" (2018) with particular benefits for young people with additional needs or who come from disadvantaged backgrounds. He recalls an experience from his time as a Head Teacher observing four hearing-impaired boys participating in the General Certificate of Secondary Education (GCSE) dance course,

> What I saw was not the boys who were deaf. They were simply the humans who danced. Liberated by movement, by that mix of creativity, self-expression and discipline that dance brings, these young men inspired the school, its staff and its pupils.
>
> (2017)

Barton's allusion here to freedom through movement speaks to growing concerns about a curriculum that is increasingly restrictive in terms of content and *modes* of learning. Some of these concerns were somewhat alleviated by the chief of Office for Standards in Education, Children's Services and Skills (Ofsted), Amanda Spielman, appealing for a "broad and rich curriculum" (2017), but it is worth noting her conception of breadth was in regard to curriculum content alone and made no mention of a curriculum broad in methodology and pedagogical practice or what Greene calls "Differentiated modes of expression" (1995, p. 17). In this publication, I argue that a curriculum focused on 'heads alone' and without regard for the fact that we do all have bodies, is a narrow and deficit curriculum. In proposing an alternative vision for a "broad and rich curriculum", I offer findings from personal research and teaching practices about what can happen when we stop focusing on heads alone and use our bodies to learn.

Embodiment

Embodiment has been defined as "the enactment of knowledge and concepts through the activity of our bodies" (Lindgren & Johnson-Glenberg, 2013, p. 445) and in the study at the heart of this book, students 'enacted' main ideas about the solar system using their bodies. Essentially, the embodiment theory is the understanding that the brain is not disconnected from the rest of the body and solely responsible for cognition, but an organ occupied with processing perceptions experienced in the body. If this were not the case, cognition would be an extremely limited mechanism for knowing the world about us, as Sanz, Gomez, Hernandez and Alarcon vividly explain, "Brains in vats are just that: brain in vats; they could produce mentality but only to the extent of the enormously limited mind-body relation that such a limited body could sustain" (2008, p. 400). The stark imagery of 'brains in vats' returns us to Robinson's observation about an education system with a narrow focus on 'heads alone' and when noted neuroscientists and philosophers draw our attention to studies which confound a binary view of mind and body (Immordino-Yang & Singh, 2011; Johnson, 2015), the message is clear – a reductive education system that ignores the role of the body in learning restricts our ability to know the world in its fullest sense.

'Knowing the world in its fullest sense' would be a fitting mission statement for the teaching of drama in schools. One of the most highly respected drama in education practitioners, Dorothy Heathcote, evoked the unique insights to be gained through drama, when she wrote that quite simply, instead of talking about an issue, "children shall think from *within* an issue" (1984, p. 119, italics added). One of the ways that students accomplish this is by assuming roles and "putting yourself into other people's shoes and, by using personal experience to help you understand their point of view, you may discover more than you knew when you started" (p. 44). However, despite the many claims about the benefits of drama that have been made over the decades, it has been argued that its diminishing presence on the school curriculum indicates research has failed to make a significant impact on educational policy (Omasta & Snyder-Young, 2014). To counteract this, drama researchers and practitioners are being urged to advocate for the impact of drama within an evidence-based framework. However, as Darlington observes, research that tracks the impact of drama on learning *over time* does not fit within an impatient educational "climate of league tables and results" (2010, p. 112). But there is hope for drama teachers, practitioners and researchers in a growing body of neuroscientific research that supports their advocacy for the unique attributes of drama as a learning medium, "What artists and educators have surmised for centuries is now the stuff of National Science Foundation grants and functional magnetic resonance imaging (fMRI) studies" (Duffy, 2014, p. 89). Artists and educators are particularly encouraged by neuroscientific research that presents learning as a physically immersive, i.e. embodied, and *affective* experience. For example, "We contend that the relationship between learning, emotion and body state runs much deeper than many educators realize" (Immordino-Yang & Damasio, 2007, p. 3). Focusing on the role of bodies specifically, Abrahamson and Lindgren state they "have everything to do with learning" (2014, p. 358) and they present the scenario of a preverbal infant sitting in the middle of a seesaw, shifting her weight around and knowing in her body the 'scientific jargon' of forces and movement that she may read about later in a school textbook. The authors also suggest "she is building an embodied sense of equivalence that will one day inform her moral reasoning about social justice" (p. 371). In other words, the value of this nonverbal and embodied learning will not only strengthen her understanding of 'scientific' principles but will cross over into broader areas of learning about life itself.

Hybrid spaces/chiasm

The idea of 'crossover' between learning experiences leads to one of the central features of the classroom study – the integration of science with drama. I have used drama in the classroom for many years, finding it to be a flexible teaching tool and yielding rich learning across the curriculum. However, science and drama may be viewed as a particular unlikely partnership (Darlington, 2010) because of traditional associations between science and fact (rationality) and drama and fiction (emotionality). Heathcote opposed such stereotyping as inaccurate and limiting,

> I've always been uncomfortable pushing art rather than, say, science, as if one were more or less imaginative or in need of brain power, than the other … . We seem to have progressed better in study skills related to object knowledge than to experience knowledge, which often is the basis of our developing world view.
>
> (1984, pp. 178–179)

Darlington views the association of science with facts alone as a missed opportunity for exploring the creativity that has played such a crucial role in scientific discoveries and problem solving (2010). Darlington, a science teacher who uses drama in her teaching, has observed how "Using a wide range of pedagogical techniques helps energise lessons through mutual enjoyment of the tasks and the positive feedback received from the pupils" (p. 109). A reluctance to employ a range of learning experiences limits opportunities for enhancing 'subject knowledge' as does an inattention to the knowledge that the students bring to school with them each day. After reporting on a study where "children's whole bodies became central, explicit tools used to accomplish the goal of representing the imaginary scientific world" (p. 320), Varelas et al. wrote, "Dramatizing creates hybrid spaces where students bring into the classroom their own everyday funds of knowledge" (2010, p. 304). These words invoke a view of learning as a fluid and overlapping dynamic between the 'outside' world and the 'classroom world'. Such a view coalesces with a theory of embodiment developed by French philosopher Maurice Merleau-Ponty. Elevating the role of our bodies in perception and rejecting the primacy of consciousness as the source of all knowing, Merleau-Ponty places the whole human body as a tool of cognition because it is the instrument through which we intertwine with the world in a phenomenon he calls "chiasm" (1968). The origin of the word is to be found in the Greek letter name 'chi', which resembles the shape of an X. In the letter X, the two lines intersect at a specific point to form the letter as we have come to know it and in ophthalmology, a chiasma refers to the intersection of the two optic pathways resulting in a singular image. Applied to the lived experience, chiasm describes an integrated existence, reconciling humans with the material world, with each other and most significantly with themselves by dismantling a mind/body binary. Merleau-Ponty describes how we are connected to all that is around us by a mirrored reversibility found in a hand that touches being touched, an eye that sees being seen and a singular body as a body among other bodies and therefore "caught in the fabric of the world" (Merleau-Ponty & Baldwin, 2004, p. 295). Through our bodily 'intertwining' with the world, we become both object and subject, a status with particular resonance for drama practices that start out a priori with bodily engagement to prime cognition, "to be, we might say, in order to think" (Osmond, 2007, p. 1109).

Drama as embodied learning

In the context of this publication, the term 'embodied learning' comprises two strands – **showing understanding through the body and strengthening cognition as a result of using the body in learning**. The idea of the body as a 'text' foregrounds this works and is based on the understanding that the body, still or in motion, carries meaning and can therefore be read (see Chapter 3). The connection between drama and the use of the body is well established. Heathcote wrote, "drama requires only a body, breathing, thinking, and feeling" (1984, p. 90) and Wagner defines drama as distinctive in its use of the body and gesture (1998). The term 'process drama' is used to describe a focus on the body as a tool for meaning. In process drama, the teacher presents aspects of the curriculum through activities that invite students to collaborate, devise and share a range of expressive responses (O'Neill, 1995). The emphasis is not on performance but in the representational particulars of the responses and how these enrich connections with curricular themes and concepts. In current education discourse, there is much debate around what constitutes a "knowledge rich curriculum" (Sherrington, 2018) and I would argue that a dramatic and embodied response is an excellent device for both representing and recording deep knowledge. The remit of process drama is to have students engage with curriculum material more actively, or as Heathcote would have it – thinking from inside a concept, not about a concept (1984) – and out of this wrestling with content to respond creatively and collaboratively. One of the conventions Heathcote devised to inspire students to think from within a problem was to cast them in the role of an expert. She carefully selected the context and the task so they would have enough knowledge from what they had been studying to assume their role as the 'ones who know' and thereby solve a dilemma. In reflecting on her method, which is known as 'mantle of the expert', Duffy writes that by "behaving *as if* the students embody the content, the experience of living within that fiction produces deeper learning" (Duffy, 2012, p. 124, italics in the original).

In contrast to learning that takes place behind a desk, process drama is an essentially dynamic mode of literacy involving physical, cognitive and emotional demands. Process drama practitioners advocate for this method of embodied learning precisely because they have witnessed how an affective engagement with curriculum leverages a strong identification with content (Duffy, 2014) and is therefore more likely to impact knowledge retention, as Giouroukakis notes here, "cognitive psychology has taught us that learners who have a sensory experience of new information retain it better" (2014, p. 27). Gee also argues for the impact on comprehension when the whole self is involved in learning, "I will argue that humans understand content, whether in a comic book or a physics text, much better when their understanding is embodied" (2004, p. 39).

In my discussion of the classroom study that was the impetus for this book, I present a range of examples to illustrate how the embodied representation and visualisation of scientific concepts strengthened the understanding about the solar system for those who devised the representations *and* those who viewed them. I also evidence how the students 'related' to abstract concepts through narrative elements and the inclusion of everyday experiences and emotions in their portrayal of scientific phenomena (see Chapter 3).

Tableau

As already mentioned, in the classroom study third grade students represented main ideas about the solar system by creating a 'tableau'. In a tableau, participants embody a key concept with motionless poses, selective gestures and carefully positioned stances. Described by Wilson as a "thinking gesture" (2003, p. 376), tableau is an established process drama technique because it affords a visual, i.e. public, and collective, i.e. group devised, depiction of a concept, theme or issue. The defining feature of a tableau is that it is a silent image, which "offers children a non-language dependent medium through which to think about ideas embedded in literature and to grow as thinkers" (Wilson, 2003, p. 375). They 'grow as thinkers' because using the body to communicate requires a physical articulacy and a precision of expression. As a non-moving but public structure, tableau requires considered attention to every part of the body – from hand gestures to the direction of gaze. As a public structure, the other students in the classroom can be invited to walk in and through the tableau, observing each carefully held posture and facial expression and interpreting what they see. This invitation brings about a heightened sense of Merleau-Ponty's intertwining of the body as subject and object – creating meaning through gestural poses and receiving meaning from those who mingle with the tableau and 'read' it as a three-dimensional text.

The absent body

The students in the classroom study had not used tableau before. According to Wee this is not surprising because "Moving the body expressively is generally not encouraged in school" (2009, p. 498) and although students are more than 'brains in vats' as referenced earlier, the dominant mode of learning in classrooms relegates the body to an appendage of learning – largely immobile and seated (Rothwell, 2011). Gee paints a vivid description of the effect this immobility has on learning, "Learning does not work well when learners are forced to check their bodies at the school room door like guns in the old West. School learning is often about disembodied minds learning outside any context of decisions and actions" (2004, p. 39).

According to John-Steiner, such physical atrophy has a deficit effect on thinking (1997) and leads to a curriculum focused on the mind and largely 'verbocentric' – a term used by Siegel to describe the elevated status accorded to words in the classroom:

> In schools, this verbocentric ideology has led us to regard language as the sole channel for learning and to separate it from other ways of knowing. The privileged status accorded to languages over images, music and movement is evident in our curriculum guides, instructional methods and materials, evaluation practices and the like.
>
> (1995, p. 456)

The attention to the body in learning is far from a new idea. In 1916, Dewey observed how a student "has a body, and brings it to school along with his mind. And the body is, of necessity, a wellspring of energy; it has to do something" (1916/1966, p. 141). And in 1967, the inspirational educator Albert Cullum wrote, "I have found that children are interested in two things – *doing* and *doing now*" (p. 15, italics in the original). 'Doing something' is of course congruent with moving the body and in Chapter 3 I attend to the active dimension of devising a tableau. One of the students in the study described the impact of *doing* on cognition when he stated, "The drama gave me more energy in my brain" and these words have remained with me as one of the most significant findings from the study and as a statement, one of the best justifications for drama in the classroom that I have encountered.

Summary

Process drama and its use of the body in learning is the antithesis of a verbocentric pedagogy. Introducing a process drama convention in the classroom begins with an act of expansion that is both literal and metaphorical, "The simple gesture of pushing back the desks in a classroom and allowing the natural creative and intellectual drives in children to flow can be the beginning of growth and an understanding of the realities of life" (Cullum, 1967, p. 21). In the context of this book, I would add that pushing back the desks created space for expanded notions of text and literacy. These expansions pushed back the limitations of a pedagogy focused on the written word alone and the restrictive practice of having students' bodies seated behind desks for long periods of time.

In researching the benefits of using the body in the classroom, I discovered three areas that were significantly impacted:

- Reading behaviour
- Cognition
- Social behaviour

The following chapters are therefore organised around each of these themes in turn and include detailed descriptions of different activities that use the body to engage with key scientific concepts related to the solar system. However, the book is more than a 'how to teach the solar system through drama' guide, and in Chapter 4, I offer additional examples of using the body as a tool for transformation in teacher education contexts. In Chapter 5, I provide further examples of using the body to teach scientific key concepts about digestion, materials and particle physics. Cumulatively, the descriptions and accounts of embodied learning that follow are inscribed with a hope that teaching will reorient a focus away from student heads alone.

References

Abrahamson, D., & Lindgren, R. (2014). Embodiment and embodied design. In R. Sawyer (Ed.), *The Cambridge handbook of the learning sciences, Cambridge handbooks in psychology* (pp. 358–376). Cambridge: Cambridge University Press. doi:10.1017/CBO9781139519526.022

Adams, R. (2017, September 21). Proportion of students taking arts subjects falls to lowest level in decade. *The Guardian*. Retrieved from: www.theguardian.com

Barton, G. (2017, September 28). Show me a great school and I'll show you a rich pulsing culture of the arts at its core. *TES*. Retrieved from: www.tes.com

Barton, G. (2018, February 27). We need to fight. Arts education is a birthright for everyone. *TES*. Retrieved from: www.tes.com/

Cullum, A. (1967). *Push back the desks*. New York: Citation Press.

Darlington, H. (2010). Teaching secondary school science through drama. *School Science Review*, *91*(337), 109–113.

Dewey, J. (1916/1966). *Democracy and education*. New York: Macmillan.

Duffy, P. (2012). Problem finders in problem spaces: A review of cognitive research for drama in education. *Youth Theatre Journal*, *26*(2), 120–132.

Duffy, P. (2014). The blended space between third and first person learning: Drama cognition and transfer. *Research in Drama Education: The Journal of Applied Theatre and Performance*, *19*(1), 89–97.

Gee, J. P. (2004). *Situated language and learning: A critique of traditional schooling*. New York: Routledge.

Giouroukakis, V. (2014, November/December). Efferent vs. aesthetic reading. *Reading Today*, *32*(1), 26–27.

Greene, M. (1995). *Releasing the imagination*. San Francisco, CA: Jossey-Bass.

Heathcote, D. (1984). *Collected writings on education and drama*, L. Johnson & C. O'Neill (Eds.), Evanston, IL: Northwestern University Press.

Immordino-Yang, M. H., & Damasio, A. R. (2007). We feel, therefore we learn: The relevance of affective and social neuroscience to education. *Mind, Brain and Education*, *1*(1), 3–10.

Immordino-Yang, M. H., & Singh, V. (2011). Perspectives from social and affective neuroscience on the design of digital learning technologies. In R. A. Calvo & S. K. D'Mello (Eds.), *New perspectives on affect and learning technologies* (pp. 233–241). New York: Springer. doi:10.1007/978-1-4419-9625-1_17

Johnson, M. (2015). Embodied understanding. *Frontiers in Psychology*, *6*(875), 1–8. doi:10.3389/fpsyg.2015.00875

John-Steiner, V. (1997). *Notebooks of the mind: Explorations of thinking*. New York: Oxford University Press.

Lindgren, R., & Johnson-Glenberg, M. (2013). Emboldened by embodiment: Six precepts for research on embodied learning and mixed reality. *Educational Researcher*, *42*(3), 445–452.

Merleau-Ponty, M. (1968). *The visible and the invisible*. Evanston, IL: Northwestern University Press.

Merleau-Ponty, M., & Baldwin, T. (2004). *Maurice Merleau-Ponty: Basic writings*. (Trans. Thomas Baldwin). London: Routledge.

Omasta, M., & Snyder-Young, D. (2014). Gaps, silences and comfort zones: Dominant paradigms in educational drama and applied theatre discourse. *Research in Drama Education: The Journal of Applied Theatre and Performance*, *19*(1), 7–22.

O'Neill, C. (1995). *Drama worlds*. Portsmouth, NH: Heinemann.

Osmond, C. R. (2007). Drama education and the body: "I am, therefore I think". In L. Bressler (Ed.), *International handbook of research in arts education. Part 2* (pp. 1109–1118). Dordrecht, the Netherlands: Springer.

Robinson, K. (2006, February). Ken Robinson: How school kills creativity [Video file]. Retrieved from: www.ted.com/talks/ken_robinson_says_schools_kill_creativity.html

Rothwell, J. (2011). Bodies and language: Process drama and intercultural language learning in a beginner language classroom. *Research in Drama Education: The Journal of Applied Theatre and Performance*, *16*(4), 575–594.

Sanz, R., Gomez, J., Hernandez, C., & Alarcon, I. (2008). Thinking with the body: Towards hierarchical, scalable cognition. In P. Calvo & A. Gomila (Eds.), *Handbook of cognitive science: An embodied approach* (pp. 395–421). Oxford, United Kingdom: Elsevier.

Sherrington, T. (2018, September). What is a knowledge rich curriculum? *Impact Journal of the Chartered College of Teaching.* Retrieved from https://impact. chartered.college/

Spielman, A. (2017, June 23). Enriching the fabric of education. Retrieved from: www.gov.uk/

Siegel, M. (1995). More than words: The generative power of transmediation for learning. *Canadian Journal of Education, 20*(4), 455–475.

Turner, C. (2017, September 21). Number of pupils taking arts subjects at GCSE falls to lowest level in a decade. *The Telegraph.* Retrieved from: www.telegraph. co.uk/

Varelas, M., Pappas, C. P., Tucker-Raymond, E., Kane, J., Hankes, J., Ortiz, I., & Keblawe-Shamah, N. (2010). Drama activities as ideational resources for primary-grade children in urban science classrooms. *Journal of Research in Science Teaching, 47*(3), 302–305. doi:10.1002/tea.20336

Wagner, B. J. (1998). *Educational drama and language arts: What research shows.* Portsmouth, NH: Heinemann.

Wee, S. J. (2009). A case study of drama education curriculum for young children in early childhood programs. *Journal of Research in Childhood Education, 23*(4), 489–501. doi:10.1080/02568540909594676

Wilson, G. P. (2003). Supporting young children's thinking through tableau. *Language Arts, 80*(5), 375–383.

2 Becoming literate

For many, the process of becoming literate would suggest progressing in the ability to read but as Greene helpfully reminds us, "There are of course many kinds of literacy" (1995, p. 25). According to Greene, 'becoming literate' equates to an expansion of thinking which leads to the provocation of imagination. In the classroom study, the composition of tableau expanded traditional modes of reading informational texts and allowed for the assimilation of imaginative ideas to represent main ideas. But what does *reading text* actually mean and more importantly, what does it actually look like in practice? The reading of a printed text comprises two facilities – attending to the written words and comprehending them. The chapter is framed by the understanding that we attend to print when we have a *purpose* for doing so and we respond to print based on our *comprehension* of content. In the description of the classroom study, the task of creating tableau gave purpose to the reading of informational texts and the tableaux became the embodied expressions of comprehension.

Expanding close reading and main idea identification

Formulating a main idea is regarded as a vital comprehension skill because students need to understand a text in order to summarise the information (Kucer, 2011). Determining the main idea of a text is a statutory guidance for reading throughout Key Stage 2 in the English National Curriculum and in the United States it is a reading target for all grade levels in the Common Core State Standards Initiative (National Governors Association, 2010). In the United States, locating the main idea is considered to be a feature of 'close reading' – the procedural analysis of text through its composite features in order to understand the meaning *in* the text. A conventional method for marking a main idea in an informational text might involve underlining the 'topic sentence' in a paragraph and circling three or four supporting details. In designing the classroom study, I wanted to redefine 'close reading' and 'identifying main idea' as practices that transcended the text itself and made space for the reader's imagination, background knowledge and body. As I considered the challenge of dramatising key concepts, I became aware of the correspondence between a main idea and a tableau. A 'main idea' is a summative statement of key concepts in a printed text and a tableau is an image composed of people holding still gestures to communicate the essence of an idea or experience (see Chapter 1). The realisation of the shared intent between a tableau and a main idea to express all that is essential about a concept was the inspiration for designing a study that involved the transfer of key content from informational text into an embodied structure – a tableau.

Transferring content across media has been called "transmediation" (Siegel, 1995; Suhor, 1984). Process drama is considered to be an ideal conduit for transmediated content because it is able to express meaning from multiple sources and in multiple ways (Wagner, 1998). According to Pearson and Fielding, transmediating content impacts comprehension and knowledge retention, "Students understand and remember ideas better when they have to transform them from one form to another. Apparently, it is in this transforming process that author's ideas become reader's ideas, rendering them more memorable" (1991, p. 847). This makes sense, for if students are involved in the transference of meaning, they are invested in both the content of what they are transferring and the process of analogising. However, transmediation is a practice which defies traditional methods of close reading because it invites the reader to consider the text from a personal standpoint alongside that of authorial intent. Close reading practices that disregard the role of the reader and the element of *affect* in the reading process are problematic for drama practices that actively encourage students to bring their "background experiences, schema knowledge, interests, desires and questions to bear on the reading of text" (Wilhelm & Edmiston, 1998, p. 33). Likewise, I saw the potential for transferring main ideas from print to tableau as an opportunity to enrich the experience of close reading by valuing what the student might bring to the science text in terms of knowledge, experience and imagination. My curiosity about the redefining of close reading by the inclusion of the body mirrored the curiosity of the following researchers as I set about designing a study focused on becoming literate through the 'three-dimensional space' of tableau, "We wonder, however, what summarizing might entail after students learned about content through means that were not only verbal but also profoundly embodied and gestural, drawing three-dimensional space into the 'meaning' of the representation" (Wilson, Boatright & Landon-Hays, 2014, p. 257).

Becoming literate

The classroom study took place during six teaching sessions over a four week period. The teaching focus was on key concepts related to a third grade (Year 4) science unit about different aspects of the solar system. See Table 2.1 for the themes of each informational text.

At the beginning of each session, a short passage of informational text was read aloud to the class. Students were then given copies of the text and assembled into groups of about four/five students. These groups remained the same for the duration of the study as did the basic structure of each session:

1   Identify a main idea
2   Write it out as a 'main idea statement'
3   Create a tableau to represent this statement
4   Present the tableau to the class

I propose these four tasks resulted in the students 'becoming literate' through:

- Purposeful reading and exploratory talk
- Efferent and aesthetic reading
- The creation of an embodied text (tableau)
- The 'reading' of an embodied text

Table 2.1 Themes of the informational texts used for each session

Texts	Themes
Text 1	The vast distance between the sun and the Earth
Text 2	Sunlight as an energy
Text 3	The gravitational pull between the sun and the Earth
Text 4	What happens during a solar eclipse
Text 5	The effects of heat from the sun
Text 6	Why the sun is important to life on Earth

Purposeful reading and exploratory talk

Aware of the association between close reading and disengaging reading practices (Snow, 2013), those who advocate for more informational texts in the classroom (e.g. Duke, 2004) have been concerned to accentuate the positive consequences of close reading informational text. When the reading results in an opportunity to present on ideas about the text to others, Fisher and Frey have noted how student reading becomes more purposeful (2014). The students in the research study knew the tableau presentation was the ultimate purpose of each session and to attain this, they took incremental purposeful steps, beginning with the rereading of the text, an important criterion of close reading. After they had reread the text, each group would begin debating the main idea of the text. Here is an extract of talk from a group as they debated the main idea of Text 1 (see Table 2.1):

Student 1: First, ok, I think the main idea is the sun.
Student 2: I think the main idea is the solar system.
Student 3: I think the main idea is like if you would want to travel to the sun or if you don't.
Student 4: Ok, this is what I was thinking, it's about how close it is but how like long it is to get there.
Student 2: We know the distance from the earth to the sun, the distance from the earth to the sun.
Student 4: Why don't we just write the main idea was the earth?
Student 3: Guys, the main idea is obvious the distance!
Student 2: Between the sun and the earth.
Student 1: What about if you want to go to the sun or not. Like it says, how far.

The energetic interchange of ideas, the acceptance of some ideas and the rejection of others are hallmarks of what Mercer calls "exploratory talk" (2008). The discourse, although a little scattered, remains focused on what they remember from the text until one student draws their attention back to the text itself with the remark "like it says". Transcripts revealed how other prompts to look back at the text were made through student comments such as "It says it in there" or "like it said in there". In one instance, a student became exasperated at her group's disagreements over the main idea and was heard saying, "let's read it and see what it's actually saying". Her concern here was very much text focused but as we shall see, students became less text bound and more open to generating their own ideas around key concepts as they began to consider their group tableau representation.

Efferent and aesthetic reading

At variance with 'close reading', Rosenblatt's seminal work "The Reader, the Text, the Poem" (1978) positions the reader at the centre of the reading experience and presents reading as an activity characterised by *efferent* and *aesthetic* reading stances, "the distinction between aesthetic and nonaesthetic reading, then, derives ultimately from what the reader does, the stance that he adopts and the activities he carries out in relation to text" (Rosenblatt, 1978, p. 27). The directives given by the students above would be an example of efferent reading because they were concerned with extracting information from the text. Aesthetic reading happens as we *bring* our own sensibilities, experiences and imagination to interact with the text and this happened as the students progressed to composing their group tableau. The audio data captured one student sharing an idea for a tableau based on Text 2 about sunlight energy,

Student: Ooh, I got an idea what we do. We should do an ice-cream truck and someone should be running after the ice-cream truck and um … And then someone should be the sun and then we just describe that it's a hot day, it's a really hot day.

The student makes a personal connection between the efferent knowledge in the text about the ability of the sun to warm objects and his experience of buying ice cream on a hot day. As an image, it conveys understanding about the sun's heat and the sensory quality of the relief an ice cream on a hot day can bring. The student applied his 'sensory experience' to tableau as evidence of comprehending the meaning of the text. Here is another example of a student verbalising a mental image based on ideas from the same text,

Student: So there's the sun who's turning the other way, so like everybody's freezing on Earth so you know how you need the sun or it would be really cold. The sun's turning this way, so the light's not facing the Earth so then everybody on the earth is freezing.

The student has extracted information from the text about the sun's essential heat energy and intertwined it with a mental picture of a sun making a deliberate act of 'turning away' from the Earth. In their final tableau presentation, the student in role as the sun made an expansive gesture of omitting light and heat *away* from the people on Earth who sat hugging themselves for warmth in the absence of the sun (see Figure 3.5). It was an aesthetic rendering of a petulant sun, choosing to direct heat away from humans and yet it encapsulated the 'main idea' of the text – that we would die without the sun's heat energy. Also of note is how different an image it is from the previous one above. Both images were based on the same text (Text 2), yet the space to incorporate 'reader's ideas' and imagination resulted in unique dramatisations that "release[d] them from the constraints of a single 'correct' interpretation" (Crumpler, 2006, p. 12). This would not have been possible through a traditional close reading analysis where justifications about meaning are made by direct references to the text itself.

The following extract of student talk conveys the dynamic interplay between efferent and aesthetic knowledge as the student combines ideas about the distance to the sun with a stylistic image of a road disappearing into the light of the sun. It epitomises Vygotsky's words about the "zigzag character of the development of fantasy and thought, which reveals itself in the 'flight' of imagination on the one hand, and its deeper reflection upon real life on the other" (1986, p. 39).

> Go to the sun, like we're all going to go to the sun, so I think it should be like there's a driver in the car and there's like a bunch, there's like one or two babies in the backseat because you know it takes so long to get to the sun and then they keep going and going and going and then there's a road, and the sun.

The 'zigzagging' of the student's imagination is interrupted momentarily by remembering the text, "you know it takes so long to get to the sun". The rapid-fire imaginings, resulting from the space to create a tableau, evoke Greene's sentiment about the rousing of imagination, "Imagination will always come into play when becoming literate suggests an opening of spaces" (Greene, 1995, p. 25). I propose this unconscious integration of efferent and aesthetic reading practices would not have occurred had the students been required to underline or highlight a main idea. Table 2.2 shows

Table 2.2 The evolution of an idea from text to tableau

Text	Student's idea	Final tableau presentation
The sun is just one of millions of stars in the sky. Why does it look bigger and brighter than any other stars? The sun looks so large and bright because it is the nearest star to Earth. It is about 150 million kilometers (93 million miles) away. If you could drive to the sun in a car, it would take you about 177 years! That is much closer than the next nearest star system, Alpha Centauri (National Geographic, 2011, p. 126).	"Go to the sun, like we're all going to go to the sun, so I think it should be like there's a driver in the car and there's like a bunch, there's like one or two babies in the backseat because you know it takes so long to get to the sun and then they keep going and going and going and then there's a road, and the sun".	

how the student's imaginative thoughts evolved into the final tableau representation of the immense distance to the sun.

These imagined scenarios are 'the stuff' of process drama and leverage opportunities for reading, comprehending and composing that enable all students to 'become literate'. Foregrounding reading opportunities with the understanding that children learn and respond in different ways opens spaces of 'becoming literate' for all students and particularly those who may be discouraged by conventional methods of literacy learning. As Patricia Wilson points out, "For children with language difficulties, talking or writing about what they know is difficult. It is easier to show what they know through tableau" (2003, p. 376). In the study, a metaphorical space for reading and responding in different ways was followed by the extension of a literal space. Desks and chairs were pushed to the side so that students were able to create a new text – tableau.

The creation of an embodied text

As a drama based, non-linear structure that emerges from group activity, tableau fulfils the call to expand literacy teaching beyond the realms of print alone (Schneider, Crumpler & Rogers, 2006). In its facility to represent meaning, tableau is a text and when those who view a tableau are invited to walk in, through and around the structure, its unique three-dimensional property affords an immediate and visceral encounter with meaning. In the context of the classroom study, tableau became an informational *and* aesthetic text comprised of bodies synchronising meaning through selective poses.

The composition of tableau undergoes a process that is distinctively collaborative (see Chapter 4) and akin to the process of written composition. The students who compose the text each bring their own ideas, imaginative capabilities and life experiences to the 'drafting' process, i.e. rehearsal of tableau. In order for the composition to be finalised, these individual contributions must be negotiated as textual components that will either concentrate meaning or detract from it. The tools of composition are the expressive attributes of the body, i.e. facial expression, hand gestures and posture (Wilson, 2003) and these can be 'experimented' with and commented upon by the others in the group until consensus is reached that the individual gestures and spacing between bodies work together in a "mutual correspondence" (Barthes, 1977, p. 70). Time-lapse images captured children manipulating their bodies into different shapes as they evolved into the gesture that was presented in their completed tableau (see Chapter 3).

The 'reading' of an embodied text

> The image arrests and detains us and commands our attention and interpretation. There is more in the tableau than a mere suspension of time. The 'perfect instant' of tableau is both totally concrete and totally abstract. In it we can read at a single glance the present, the past and the future – in other words the complete meaning of the represented action.
>
> (O'Neill, 1995, p. 127)

Conceptualising tableau as a text strengthens the spectatorship of tableau as an act of reading. When a tableau is presented by a group of students in the classroom, an initial reading can be elicited by asking the spectating students 'What do you see?' This opening question, requiring a studied overview of the *whole* image, draws attention to the overall message of the image and parallels an initial 'read through' of the text. After hearing the students' suggestions, students can be asked to comment on the particulars of the compositional devices in a process analogous to Fisher's description of close reading, "When we have students really read carefully, they pay attention to the words, the ideas, the structure, the flow, and the purpose of that text" (McGraw-Hill Education, 2012). Although Fisher was referencing the close reading of a written document, the result of closely analysing textual features is the same as with a tableau – studying the "performative gestures" (Wilson, 2003, p. 377) in a tableau develops the skill of reading movements, feelings, motivations and intentions that are captured in stillness and intended as expressions of meaning.

Developing inferential reading skills can be applied to reading a tableau by asking reader response type questions such as 'how do you know?' or 'what makes you think that?' In answering these queries, students are invited to make specific reference to the 'performative gestures' in the tableau. However, these questions also draw upon student background knowledge and interpretive skills as they make links between what they see before them and what they bring to the seeing of tableau. In other words, the prompts maintain focus on the content of the tableau while opening a space for student exposition of text (Branscombe, 2015). The arts slow us down and make us look – closely. As a distilled image, tableau has no past or future. It is truly of the moment and in the act of contemplating an image, Merleau-Ponty claims we experience atemporality. "The present still holds on to the immediate past without positing it as an object, and since the immediate past similarly holds its immediate predecessor, past time is wholly collected up and grasped in the present" (2004, p. 82). As an embodied 'grasp' in the present, tableau has the potential to root the viewer in the present and momentarily relieve them of time constraints, a novel experience in today's world.

Summary

An important element of 'becoming literate' involves developing as readers and composers of text. In the context of this chapter, the purpose of creating a tableau made space for both outcomes. Arising out of imagination, tableau reoriented the reading of informational text to become more than the identification of main ideas. The composition of tableau meant students transformed efferent knowledge into an aesthetic structure. When the tableaux were presented to the other students, they became texts to be read and the augmentation of meaning by student interpretation expanded traditional conceptions of 'close reading' beyond print-based documents.

References

Barthes, R. (1977). *Image music text*. New York: Hill and Wang.

Branscombe, M. (2015). Showing not telling: Tableau as an embodied text. *The Reading Teacher, 69*(3), 321–329.

Crumpler, T. P. (2006). Educational drama as response to literature: Possibilities for young learners. In J. J. Schneider, T. P. Crumpler, & T. Rogers (Eds.), *Process drama and multiple literacies* (pp. 1–14). Portsmouth, NH: Heinemann.

Duke, N. K. (2004). The case for informational text. *Educational Leadership, 61*(6), 40–44.

Fisher, D., & Frey, N. (2014). Closely reading informational texts in the primary grades. *The Reading Teacher, 68*(3), 222–227. doi:10.1002/trtr.1317

Greene, M. (1995). *Releasing the imagination*. San Francisco, CA: Jossey-Bass.

Kucer, S. B. (2011). Processing expository discourses: What factors predict comprehension? *Reading Psychology, 32*(6), 567–583.

McGraw-Hill Education. (2012). *Douglas Fisher: Close reading and the CCSS, part 1*. Retrieved from: www.youtube.com/watch?v=5w9v6-zUg3Y

Mercer, N. (2008). *Three Kinds of Talk*. [PDF file]. Retrieved from: https://thinkingtogether.educ.cam.ac.uk/resources/5_examples_of_talk_in_groups.pdf

Merleau-Ponty, M. & Baldwin, T. (2004). *Maurice Merleau-Ponty: Basic writings* (Trans. Thomas Baldwin). London: Routledge.

National Geographic. (2011). *National Geographic science grade 3 teacher's edition earth science – Florida 1E*. Heinle/ELT, a part of Cengage Learning Inc.

National Governors Association Center for Best Practices & Council of Chief State School Officers. (2010). *Common core state standards*. Washington, DC: Authors.

O'Neill, C. (1995). *Drama worlds*. Portsmouth, NH: Heinemann.

Pearson, P. D., & Fielding, L. (1991). Comprehension instruction. In R. Barr, M. L. Kamil, P. Mosenthal, & P. D. Pearson (Eds.), *Handbook of reading research* (Vol. II), (pp. 815–860). White Plains, NY: Longman.

Rosenblatt, L. (1978). *The reader, the text, the poem*. Carbondale, IL: Southern Illinois University Press.

Schneider, J. J., Crumpler, T. P., & Rogers, T. (Eds.). (2006). *Process drama and multiple literacies*. Portsmouth, NH: Heinemann.

Siegel, M. (1995). More than words: The generative power of transmediation for learning. *Canadian Journal of Education, 20*(4), 455–475.

Snow, C. E. (2013, June 6). Cold versus warm close reading: Stamina and the accumulation of misdirection [Web log post]. Retrieved from: www.literacy worldwide.org/blog/literacy-daily/2013/06/06/cold-versus-warm-close-reading-stamina-and-the-accumulation-of-misdirection

Suhor, C. (1984). Towards a semiotics-based curriculum. *Journal of Curriculum Studies, 16*(3), 247–257.

Vygotsky, L. S. (1986). *Thought and language*. Cambridge, MA: The MIT Press.

Wagner, B. J. (1998). *Educational drama and language arts: What research shows*. Portsmouth, NH: Heinemann.

Wilhelm, J. D., & Edmiston, B. (1998). *Imagining to learn*. Portsmouth, NH: Heinemann.

Wilson, A. A., Boatright, M. D., & Landon-Hays, M. (2014). Middle school teachers' discipline-specific use of gestures and implications for disciplinary literacy instruction. *Journal of Literacy Research, 46*(2), 234–262.

Wilson, G. P. (2003). Supporting young children's thinking through tableau. *Language Arts, 80*(5), 375–383.

3   Embodied cognition

When the students were asked if tableau helped them understand main ideas about the solar system, one student wrote, "Yes, it gave me more energy in my brain". These words speak of cognition primed by activity and allude to the synergy between bodily experience and neurological process as reported in recent neuroscientific research and discussed in Chapter 1. In this chapter, the student's simple yet profound response provides the basis for examining the tableaux as evidence of energised brains grappling with abstract ideas and representing key concepts *through the use of the body*. I name this outcome 'embodied comprehension' and focus on *role* and *gesture* as the embodied devices used by the students to make abstract concepts concrete and thereby show their understanding. I also consider the integration of narrative structures in the tableaux as supporting key concepts and I highlight the role of creativity in going beyond the 'humdrum' of classroom life and making learning memorable.

Study synopsis

The students in the study were exposed to six sessions of learning about the solar system. Each session was similarly structured: students worked in groups to read a passage of informational text about the solar system (see Table 2.1)[1], reach consensus on a key concept, write the key concept *in their own words* as a 'main idea statement' and then embody this statement in a static image known as a tableau (see Chapter 1 for a more detailed description of tableau). Each group member was required to be in the tableau so that it represented a *collective* understanding of a main idea.

Tableau data

Time-lapse images were recorded as the students created their tableaux. Final tableau presentations were photographed and additional pictures taken that isolated gestures, expressions and spatial positioning of 'bodies'. When presenting the tableau, the participants were asked to identify their role and these role choices were documented. At the end of session 4 and 6, students were asked to write from the perspective of the role they had just enacted in a tableau. These 'writing in role' compositions provided further insights into the concept of roles as agents embodying key concepts within a tableau structure. Finally, students were asked to write down their opinions about the value of tableau to learn scientific content.

Embodied cognition through role, gesture and narrative

Role

In a tableau, meaning is made by each participant assuming a role and in the study after each group had decided on a main idea they were going to represent in a tableau, the next decision was about the role each student would 'play'. Role taking is a heightened experience of Merleau-Ponty's duality of perception, for through "role taking, individuals are simultaneously positioned as knowers and nonknowers, insiders and outsiders" (Branscombe & Schneider, 2018, p. 21), and in Chapter 4, I discuss the affordance of having an inside perspective as one that leads to transformation of perception.

When the groups presented their tableaux, the participants announced their role and this became valuable data for analysing the degree of connection with the informational source text. Using the documentation of student roles, I categorised role according to 'type' and counted the frequency of types of role (see Table 3.1).

The informational texts used for the majority of the sessions were based on a unit about Earth science and the solar system in a science textbook, therefore the high frequency of roles depicting space objects was to be expected. The sun featured prominently in all six texts and was a popular role to play. The declaration "I want to be the sun" was often heard as students planned their tableaux.

Gesture

Roles are defined by gesture, with hands, posture and positioning as devices communicating emotion, intent, activity, status and relationship to other

Table 3.1 Types of role and the frequency of their depiction in the six sessions

Type of role and examples	Frequency
Space objects – sun, moon, Earth, stars, asteroids, meteors and planets ('objects' is the term used in the Next Generation of Science Standards (www.nextgenscience.org/next-generation-science-standards)	43
People (e.g. astronauts, singer, mom, baby)	33
Animals and plants (e.g. cockroach, bird, flower)	12
Energy sources and forces (e.g. heat, light, gravity)	9
Earth bound objects (e.g. truck, tower, ball)	7
Total number of roles in six sessions	104

roles (Branscombe & Schneider, 2013). Therefore, these "focal points" (Wilson, 2003, p. 378) became the focus analysing indications of cognition about main ideas related to the informational texts.

Hands

The gestural use of hands was a major signifier in the embodied representations of 'space objects' and when in the role as the sun, the stretching of arms and hands away from the body, and the resulting expansion of the body either vertically or horizontally, was integral to almost *every* representation (see Figure 3.1). This commonality in the expressive use of hands is an example of what Wilson calls a "culturally established gesture" (2003, p. 378) and Barthes defines as a "universal symbolic order" (1977, p. 18), a "historical grammar" (p. 22) and an "iconographic connotation" (p. 22). When attending to the connotation of an icon, Barthes directs us to "look for its material in painting, theatre, associations of ideas, stock metaphors, etc., that is to say precisely in 'culture'" (p. 22). In religion, mythology, art and science the sun is a dominating, life-giving symbol and in these choices of gesture and often centralised positions, students evidenced their understanding of the sun as the dominant presence in the solar system and the sustainer of all that revolves around it.

At times, the sun became an even bigger presence in a tableau when *pairs* of students formed a singular representation. These collaborative representations also evidenced a successful outcome of students working together as part of the creative process (see Chapter 4). In these paired structures, one student stood behind the other but both students had their arms pointing in different positions. These paired representations caused

Figure 3.1 Student representations of the sun.

the sun to be even more dominant in the tableau and effectively conveyed main ideas about the sun as a source of intense heat and light (see Figure 3.2).

Hands were also used to represent a source of energy or a force. For the text about gravity, students who depicted 'gravity' as a role held their hands away from their body and gestured the emission of a force. One group decided on their main idea sentence as "The energy the sun gives off". For their tableau, two students sat at ground level and stretched their fingers, hands and legs forwards to denote their roles as "streams of energy" (see Figure 3.3).

Posture

Students used height to posture the status of their role. The largeness of the sun often contrasted with the smaller postures of those in other roles and showed an understanding of the sun as the largest object in the solar system. In Figure 3.4, the student on the left represented the sun by stretching her

Figure 3.2 Pairs of students combined individual asymmetrical gestures to form symmetrical representations of the sun.

Figure 3.3 Students used outstretched arms and hands to represent energy or force.

hands above her head and standing on a chair to make herself even taller and thereby signify the sun's magnitude. The student on the right was also in the role as the sun but in contrast to the usual portrayal of the sun, she used a downward orientation of her hands, head and shoulders to portray a sun no longer emitting any heat. This was in response to Text 6 that considered what life would be like without the sun. The main idea statement written by this group was "no sun so everything's dying out".

In another tableau where students showed what would happen on Earth if the sun no longer shone, one student in the role as the sun stood with an

Figure 3.4 Contrasting images of the sun through posture.

Figure 3.5 The sun's reversed posture denies life to the humans on Earth.

expansive but flattened posture, as if she had become a two-dimensional picture book version of her former three-dimensional powerhouse capability. She had her back turned on "the freezing cold people" who, in contrast, showed their suffering status with kneeling and huddled postures (see Figure 3.5).

In contrast to the iconic representations of the sun as an all-powerful force, the Earth was often portrayed as an inferior, sometimes comical object, subject to the whims of the sun. In a tableau about the sun's gravitational pull on the Earth (Text 3), the sun stood on a chair with arms raised high and looked down on an Earth who posed as if attempting to run away from the sun. It was a humorous image and reminiscent of a misbehaving cartoon character running on the spot whilst being held in place by a character with much greater strength – gravity. The student in the role as 'gravity' stretched her entire body between the sun and the Earth, resting her feet on the chair of the sun and almost touching the Earth with an outstretched hand. Her elongated body served to represent the gravitational force that binds Earth and sun together (see Figure 4.1 in Chapter 4).

Positioning

Students used positioning to denote main ideas and/or information about their roles in relation to other roles. I examined students' positioning in the tableaux along a spectrum of 'closeness' to each other. Proximity was used to signify connectivity between roles based on ideas to be found in the texts. In a tableau about the gravitational force between the sun and the Earth, students used positioning in ways that reflected iconic representations of villains and victims. Each role in the tableau resembled a character from an action movie. Two students in the role as 'gravity' stood either side of, and very close to, the sun (the villain), as if they were the sun's 'heavies'. The Earth lay on the floor in front of them and in a tightly curled posture as if it had been beaten up. Given the text was about the Earth depending on gravity to keep it from 'falling into the sun', it was a depiction of an Earth relegated to a position of servitude (see Figure 3.6).

The idea of transference through physical contact was evident in many of the tableaux. In tableaux where students were physically (or very nearly) connected, the students positioned in the middle were the conduit of a force or energy. In a tableau based around the main idea sentence, "The energy the sun gives off", two "streams of energy" positioned themselves between the sun and the Earth. The sun's expansive pose indicated its power as the source of the energy streams. The student in role as the Earth positioned himself on the same level as the streams of energy and faced the energy/sun/energy trio as if happy to accept and receive the transfer of heat energy from the sun (see Figure 3.7).

Figure 3.6 Students used high and low positions to denote status.

Figure 3.7 Students took up middle positions to denote the role of a conduit.

Text 4 was about what happens during a solar eclipse. Students depicted the phenomenon with roles representing the key astronomical 'objects'. Tableaux featured a moon blocking the sun but the positioning and blocking gestures differed between groups (see Figure 3.8).

In one tableau, the outstretched rays of the sun could be seen behind the moon, but the shy smile on the face of the moon who stood in front of the sun suggested a moment of triumph. The other two students in the tableau took on roles as people responding to this sudden darkness – one as a "guy holding a flashlight" and the other student in role as an "OMG person". She opened her eyes wide and put a hand to her mouth, expressing both fear and wonderment at the spectacle unfolding before her. Another group also had the moon standing in front of a sun who effectively portrayed a diminished power with hands bound together over her head rather than the customary 'arms – stretched – out' gesture. Once again, a smile on the face of the moon spoke of conquest. The other three students in the tableau crouched at varying distances from the moon and between them depicted two surprised girls peeping at the eclipse from behind a chair, and a "disappointed bird". This choice of role was in response to the information in the text about birds who "think it's night time and stop singing" and it evidenced the student had paid attention to what a close reading analysis would call a 'supporting detail' for a main idea. A traditional classroom, and seat-bound, activity may have required him to underline such details but I propose taking on the role of a bird disappointed at not being able to sing is a more effective practice

Figure 3.8 Students used different gestures to block the sun in portrayals of a solar eclipse.

in helping a student remember *specific* impacts of a solar eclipse on the natural world.

One group chose completely different stances and positioning to represent the overshadowing of the sun by the moon. A student in role as the sun lay flat on his back on the floor, with an expression of terror while the moon arched over him, effectively in a gesture of entrapment. The Earth was positioned closely behind the moon and peering out into the distance as if it was struggling to look at something. The personification of the sun as an impotent being, tormented by a suffocating moon and expedient earth, was an aesthetic rendering of an eclipse as the ultimate inversion of the natural order – which is surely the main idea of an eclipse. The apocalyptic mood was intensified by the close positioning between the three roles, making it a very claustrophobic image to view. It was the embodied fusing of efferent and aesthetic reading stances (see Chapter 2) and an effective use of bodies to show understanding.

When students placed themselves far away from each other in a tableau, I attended closely to the roles. In one tableau, a student in role as an astronaut placed herself in an isolated position but her crouched posture behind a chair denoted her diminutive size in comparison to the stars, and her peeping over the top of the chair suggested she was fearful of getting too close. As a major presence in many of the texts, the sun's importance was sometimes shown in the tableaux through other roles keeping their distance so that our attention as spectators was drawn to the sun. The isolated positioning of roles showing death or suffering (based on ideas from Text 6) reinforced a lack of human contact as contributing to a sense of doom and hopelessness. Frightened, suffering characters occupied solitary spaces and avoided eye contact with others, preferring to stare "into space" and "hug" themselves (see Figure 3.9).

Figure 3.9 Students used isolated positioning to show death and suffering.

People roles

The frequency of roles representing people was significant because humans were not explicitly referenced in any of the texts. In addition, 'people roles' became increasingly descriptive as the study progressed with the students adding adjectives to their reported roles. In the first session based on a text about the distance between the Earth and the sun, a total of two people roles were depicted and described by the students as "driver" and "baby in the back seat" (in the tableau, the baby lay on the backseat of the car, clutching his knees and crying in despair at the never-ending journey to the sun. You can see the image in Table 2.2). Tableaux based on Text 6 (about the importance of the sun for life on Earth) had a variety of people roles and the students gave these roles the following descriptors: frozen guy, frozen teenager, frightened girl, frozen person, frozen lawyer, a man dying, guy trying to open coffee, a mommy helping her son, a frozen baby, dying person, dead lady. The use of adjectives, emotions and actions to describe characters in the tableaux indicated how the students were imbuing people roles with background stories and relationships.

Narrative in tableau

By adding human activity and relational dimensions to an efferent reading of the informational text, students were infusing narrative patterns that evidenced "human elements, such as feelings, attitudes, actions and behaviors towards each other and towards the entities they pretend to be" (Varelas et al., 2010, p. 317). This narrativisation of text also returns us to the idea in Chapter 2 of the study as an integration of Rosenblatt's efferent and aesthetic reading stances (Rosenblatt, 1978). The students were endowing key efferent concepts with affective responses embedded in narratives, relational constructs and emotional states springing from imagination and background knowledge. Eliciting background knowledge is an established comprehension practice (Pohlman, 2008) and in this instance it proved to be a fertile mechanism for generating metaphors around important concepts. Tableaux mediated and were mediated by abstract ideas that became grounded in experiences the students themselves had lived. One tableau featured a scene of buying ice cream on a hot day to represent the concept of sunlight as a warming energy that can make us feel overheated and in need of relief (Text 2). These experiences came into focus as episodes that could have resided in stories with titles such as "The Hot Day" or "The Day the

Sun Died". Alternatively, they could have been used as prompts for poems, stories or devised plays; the point being that it is possible to extend informational text into opportunities for blurring binary constructs between information and fiction, science and drama, abstract and concrete, efferent and aesthetic. We create narratives by living each day, or as Johnson writes, "the very pattern of human experience is narrative" (1989, p. 372). Encountering scientific phenomena is an inherent part of our everyday lived experience, therefore it would seem only 'natural' that narrative should be a part of learning science and making science learning known.

Writing in role

In the study, tableau was the outcome of engaging with informational texts, however, in sessions 4 and 6, the experience of being in a tableau was also used as a "concrete reference to spark writing activities" (Tortello, 2004, p. 207). 'Writing in role' is written from the perspective of an insider's experience. Having been in role means students have a pretext (O'Neill, 1995) for imaginative writing that voices a character's intent, motivation and emotional state. This concrete frame of reference particularly assists students who struggle to initiate writing (McKean & Sudol, 2002) or students who are English Language Learners (Brouilette, 2013).

Student writing in role responses

The written compositions varied from the very factual, "I was the sun and the moon was blocking me" to the more reflexive, "As the sun in the eclipse I was sad because I didn't get to do my part, I didn't get to shine in the day, only at the end" (see Figure 3.10).

One student in role as the sun expressed indignation at what was happening, "I was the sun. I thought like the sun should not be blocked". We know that space objects don't have feelings, but the appropriateness of having the sun express humiliation at being covered by the Earth and the effect of attributing human emotions to space objects made the student writing engaging and provided evidence of student understanding of scientific concepts. It was in Duffy's words "a palimpsest of content transfer" (2014, p. 92). Duffy describes the shift in writing *about* an event to writing from *inside* an event as a transfer from 'third to first person learning' (2014). Third person learning is characterised by a sense of distance from the curricular material whereas first person learning blends curriculum information with

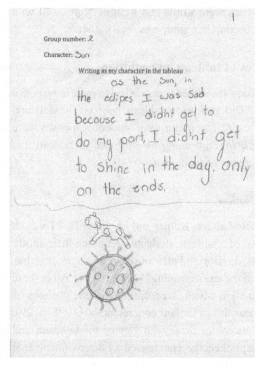

Group number: 2

Character: Sun

Writing as my character in the tableau

as the Sun, in the eclipes I was sad becouse I didn't get to do my part, I didn't get to shine in the day, only on the ends.

Figure 3.10 Student writing in role compositions.

experiences students have lived and emotions they have felt. After session 4 and writing from the Earth's perspective, one sample carried the tone of a gossipy anecdote being shared with a friend, "I was having a hot day but not too hot. But then it got dark. I looked at the sun but in front of it was the moon. I said it's cold, can you move over? And he did". Likewise, in another writing in role response, the moon's 'voice' was personified through a celebratory tone of triumph and elation, "In the tableau I was thinking, wow, it took 100 years to get in front of the sun, but I did it. I'm in front" and "I felt happy because now everyone can see me! Yay!" Responses written from the voice of a human in a tableau captured the confusion caused by a solar eclipse. "What is that?" asked a student in role as a small girl looking at the eclipse, while another student wrote in the style of an inner monologue, "My thoughts were … why was the sky black and dark? It was mostly always light. Is it night-time? Did I just didn't notice it [sic]?" and after session 6, words written from the perspective of a mother comforting her dying son in a world absent of sunlight were highly emotional, "It's ok sweetie, I'll die with you". They were words that went perfectly well with the role and gesture she had used in her group's tableau earlier.

Analysing the affordances of tableau on cognition

At the end of the classroom study, the students were asked to write in response to the following question, "Did making a tableau help you understand the main idea of a science text?" The majority of student responses were positive and indicated *visualising* and *doing* as attributes of tableau that most strengthened comprehension of main ideas.

Comprehension and visualisation

In support of the findings noted above, Kelner and Flynn write, "Through the planning and presentation of a tableau, students strengthen their ability to visualize the written words, develop and present sensory images, and thus gain a deeper understanding of the text's meaning" (2006, p. 151). All of these elements arose out of imagination which, according to Greene, "allows us to particularize, to see and hear things in their concreteness" (1995, p. 29). This theory also has implications for those who viewed the tableaux and saw abstract scientific concepts become concretised as three-dimensional images. Darlington touches on this aspect of drama in science teaching when she writes how it can "make the concepts being studied, such as particle models, diffusion and materials, seem more real to the pupils rather than remote theoretical concepts" (2010, p. 111).

Visualising content has long been recognised as an important skill in enabling students to access the meaning of text. When embedded as a mental imprint, the argument follows that meaning can be retained and therefore retrieved more effectively (Long, Winograd & Bridge, 1989). Visualising as a comprehension tool has traditionally been taught by encouraging students to mentally imagine content or having them record important ideas and concepts in visual representations that are known by various labels, e.g. concept maps, graphic organisers, mind maps, relationship charts. In science, teachers make frequent use of concept maps and models as pedagogical tools for visualising and analogising processes that cannot be seen in situ or are abstracted from our everyday experiences. These analogies come in different formats but are rarely composed of human bodies and the act of dramatising phenomena in the form of a model remains underutilised despite research that orients drama as a representational medium for making "thinking more explicit" (McGregor, 2012, p. 1161) and knowable through analogy, metaphor and story (Shanahan & Nieswandt, 2009).

Tableau as an embodied concept map

A simple comparison between a tableau and a traditional concept map is made here to warrant its description as an *embodied* concept map. In a traditional concept map, key terms are given nodal prominence and are linked to other key terms by connecting arrows to denote connections of process. There is no superfluous information other than what is needed to communicate the essence of a particular event. Likewise, a tableau is a structure denoting the essence of an event and composed of individual bodies holding static gestures as nodes of meaning and intent. These individual bodies show a schematic relationship to other bodies through careful positioning and expressions of connectedness, e.g. eye contact, touch, proximity. The placement of isolated bodies in a tableau is a deliberate device to denote disconnect or to draw attention to them for a particular reason. For example, in the classroom tableaux, the sun was often isolated but dominant in its isolation through expansive gestures which signified its importance in the solar system. Similarly, a concept map of the solar system would likely have the sun in the centre and surrounded by the planets in orbit formation. However, an important distinction between a concept map and a tableau is that drama "shorten[s] the distance between object of study and subject, providing a more holistic experiential approach to learning science" (Varelas et al., 2010, p. 322). I would add the word 'immersive' to this affordance; those who create the image and its meaning are fully immersed in the meaning which therefore increases their affective experience of information. In the dramatic form of tableau, the body holds its identity as subject/object in tension, simultaneously aware of the need to embody meaning in order to represent meaning and as such a duality of 'seeing' results – creating from within while simultaneously envisioning what it looks like from without (Merleau-Ponty, 1968). According to Duke and Pearson,

> The point about visual representations is that they are re-presentations; literally, they allow us to present information again. It is through that active, transformative process that knowledge, comprehension, and memory form a synergistic relationship – whatever improves one of these elements also improves the others.
>
> (2002, p. 219)

Tableau and 'doing'

Research reports on the teaching of science through drama include studies involving the body to replicate the rapid back and forth actions of sound waves (Hendrix, Eick & Shannon, 2012), mimic positively charged atoms (Alrutz, 2004) and dramatise animal activities associated with the construction of a food web (Varelas et al., 2010). When these research findings are synthesised, they reflect Vygotsky's theory of learning becoming meaningful through doing (Vygotsky, 1978).

When asked if tableau had helped the students understand the main idea of a science text, activity became an important theme and present in answers that included words such as "making", "doing" and "acting". One student wrote, "it helped me by acting them out and that I felt like I really was that thing". Such responses support research which connects meaning to action and the role of the body in strengthening cognitive functioning (Block, Parris & Whiteley, 2008; Glenberg, Jaworski & Rischal, 2007; Lindgren & Johnson-Glenberg, 2013; Sadoski, 2009). The students communicated how an energised brain was an engaged brain and an engaged brain, as Lindgren and Johnson-Glenberg tell us, is a brain open to the development of new knowledge. "If physical movement *primes* mental constructs, such as language, then it may be that increasing an individual's repertoire of conceptually grounded physical movement will provide fertile areas from which new knowledge structures can be developed" (2013, p. 446, italics in the original).

Although a tableau is a still structure, it evolves through movement and students trying out different gestures. In the study, to embody the main idea was to be actively involved in its representation through both the planning and the presentation of tableau. The students arrived at the final outcome of tableau through a devising process that moved from text centred to 'body centred'. A time-lapse camera was set up in the corner of the classroom and captured important data about the "flow, patterns and shapes of movement" (Kozel, 2007, p. 220) during sessions. Students began their preparation of tableau in clustered groups, drawn together by copies of the text for the session, the sheet on which they wrote their 'main idea sentence' and the purpose of discussing the text to identify a main idea (see Figure 3.11).

Regarding the presence of circular shapes in classrooms, Branscombe and Schneider have observed that, "Bodies, positioned in circular shapes, became the semiotic sign for a community of learners" (2018, p. 16). The

Figure 3.11 Students begin clustered around the information texts.

time-lapse images show how after a time, the clustered shape patterns broke apart as the students practiced their tableau, tried out different ideas and consulted with each other.

As groups broke out from their clustered working patterns to begin practicing their final tableau presentations, there were observable changes in body patterns. When students stood around their tables at the beginning of their collaborative deliberations over text, their arms were at their sides and their heads were downwards. As they broke away from proximity to the 'discussion' table, body shapes became more varied as they experimented with different heights, postures and gestures. The time-lapse images recorded students experimenting with different shapes. Images of one student capture her trying out her role as a star; in one image she has one arm stretching upwards but in the next image she has both arms raised. In the final tableau, she has reverted back to having one arm raised and the other arm pointing downwards. Her shifting choices echo a dynamic found in the following statement, "[tableau's] most important contribution to comprehension may be that they allow readers to be active and generative" (Tortello, 2004, p. 207). These active experimentations showed the evolution of ideas that were actualised in the final tableau photographs and in effect the time-lapse photographs were the tracings of a collaborative product (see Table 3.2).

Table 3.2 The evolution of a tableau

Time-lapse photographs of 10 second intervals	*Observations*
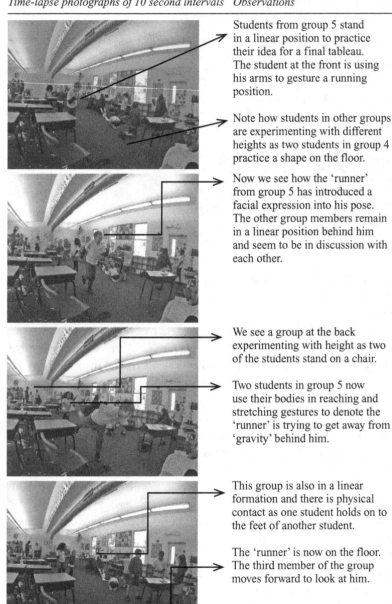	Students from group 5 stand in a linear position to practice their idea for a final tableau. The student at the front is using his arms to gesture a running position. Note how students in other groups are experimenting with different heights as two students in group 4 practice a shape on the floor. Now we see how the 'runner' from group 5 has introduced a facial expression into his pose. The other group members remain in a linear position behind him and seem to be in discussion with each other. We see a group at the back experimenting with height as two of the students stand on a chair. Two students in group 5 now use their bodies in reaching and stretching gestures to denote the 'runner' is trying to get away from 'gravity' behind him. This group is also in a linear formation and there is physical contact as one student holds on to the feet of another student. The 'runner' is now on the floor. The third member of the group moves forward to look at him.

Table 3.3 focuses on the creative process of one group in particular and is useful in its recording of shifting decisions about gesture and student participation. It also records moments of student collaboration and adjustment of each other's gestures.

Table 3.3 Group 4 experiments with different body shapes and students for their final tableau

Time-lapse screen shot	Observation
	The image shows two students as they practice representing a solar eclipse.
	Another member of the group appears in the paired image and a new image is created with different body patterns.
	The two students standing one behind the other represent the moon (in the front) and the sun (behind). The student on the left is practicing his gesture as someone "holding a flashlight". The image gets closer to the tableau presentation (see final image).

(*Continued*)

Table 3.3 Continued

Time-lapse screen shot	Observation
	The 'moon' has changed her hands to be arched above her head. The sun's posture remains the same.
	Note how another group member seems to be adjusting the shape of the 'flashlight holder'.
	Photograph* of final tableau presentation about a solar eclipse. The student on the left represents an "OMG human".

* Not a time-lapse image.

Disrupting the routine of classroom learning

As the images above testify, creating tableau is an active and expressive process that disrupts the routine of traditional classroom practice. It needs space in many forms – physical space for experimenting with different gestures and an ideological space for accepting the creative process may not always resemble 'learning' narrowly defined. The classroom became very noisy at times and student interactions were not always focused on the task of creating tableau (see Chapter 4). However, for the most part they were engaged students enjoying the opportunity to "shed those roles that others assign them (e.g. that of *child*, *student* or *pupil*)" (Heath & Wollach, 2008, p. 6, italics in the original). The opportunity to be someone or something else is a novel experience in an environment where you are traditionally expected to perform as a student and not a "disappointed bird" or "a mother" comforting her son because the world is coming to a catastrophic end. The creation of tableau was a literacy practice extending the experience of reading informational text into imaginative and playful spaces. We need to provide space for innovative learning practices if we are to disrupt the routine of classroom learning and keep students engaged, "in the everyday life that surrounds us, creativity is an essential condition for existence and all that goes beyond the rut of routine and involves innovation" (Vygotsky, 2004, p. 11). In an era of narrowing curricula and high stakes testing, we need to be more intentional than ever about including learning experiences that go 'beyond the rut of routine'. These learning experiences do not have to be based on time consuming or fantastical ideas because as Heathcote reminds us, the remit of drama is to "make ordinary experiences significant" (1984, p. 24). It is work of *significance* that Heathcote believes students crave the most, "The ones I meet are not asking for less work, or easier work, they are asking for more meaningful work" (p. 30). I believe the beauty of tableau lies with its simple design (no costumes, no props), and yet this simplicity enables an attention to ideas of significance.

Note

1 Frequent references to the informational texts occur throughout this chapter. Table 2.1 summarises the themes of the informational texts.

References

Alrutz, M. (2004). Granting science a dramatic license: Exploring a 4th grade science classroom and the possibilities for integrating drama. *Teaching Artist Journal, 2*(1), 31–39.

Barthes, R. (1977). *Image music text.* New York: Hill and Wang.

Block, C. C., Parris, S. R., & Whiteley, C. S. (2008). CPMs: A kinesthetic comprehension strategy. *The Reading Teacher, 61*(6), 460–470.

Branscombe, M., & Schneider, J. (2018). Accessing teacher candidates' pedagogical intentions and imagined teaching futures through drama and arts-based structures. *Action in Teacher Education, 40*(1), 19–37.

Branscombe, M., & Schneider, J. (2013). Embodied discourse: Using tableau to explore preservice teachers' reflections and activist stances. *Journal of Language and Literacy Education, 9*(1), 48–65. Retrieved from: http://jolle.coe.uga.edu/volume-91-2013/

Brouilette, L. (2013). Advancing the speaking and listening skills of K – 2 English language learners through creative drama. *TESOL Journal, 3*(1), 138–145.

Darlington, H. (2010). Teaching secondary school science through drama. *School Science Review, 91*(337), 109–113.

Duffy, P. (2014). The blended space between third and first person learning: Drama cognition and transfer. *Research in Drama Education: The Journal of Applied Theatre and Performance, 19*(1), 89–97.

Duke, N. K., & Pearson, P. D. (2002). Effective practices for developing reading comprehension. In A. E. Farstrup & S. J. Samuels (Eds.), *What research has to say about reading instruction* (3rd ed., pp. 205–242), Newark, DE: International Reading Association.

Glenberg, A. M., Jaworski, B., & Rischal, M. (2007). What brains are for: Action, meaning and reading comprehension. In D. S. McNamara (Ed.), *Reading comprehension strategies: Theories, interventions and technologies* (pp. 221–240). Marwah, N.J.: Lawrence Erlbaum Associates, Inc.

Greene, M. (1995). *Releasing the imagination.* San Francisco, CA: Jossey-Bass.

Heath, S. B., & Wollach, R. (2008). Vision for learning: History, theory and affirmation. In J. Flood, S. B. Heath & D. Lapp (Eds.), *Handbook for literacy educators: Research in the visual and communicative arts.* Vol. 2. pp. 3–12, New York: Lawrence Erlbaum.

Heathcote, D. (1984). Excellence in teaching. In L. Johnson & C. O'Neill, (Eds.), *Collected writings on education and drama.* Evanston, IL: Northwestern University Press.

Hendrix, R., Eick, C., & Shannon, D. (2012). The integration of creative dramatics in an inquiry-based elementary program: The effect on student attitude and conceptual learning. *Journal of Science Teacher Education, 23,* 823–846. doi:10.1007/s10972-012-9292-1

Johnson, M. (1989). Embodied knowledge. *Curriculum Inquiry, 19*(4), 361–377.

Kelner, L. B., & Flynn, R. (2006). *A dramatic approach to reading comprehension: Strategies and activities for classroom teachers.* Portsmouth, NH: Heinemann.

Kozel, S. (2007). *Closer.* Cambridge, MA: The MIT Press.

Lindgren, R., & Johnson-Glenberg, M. (2013). Emboldened by embodiment: Six precepts for research on embodied learning and mixed reality. *Educational Researcher, 42*(3), 445–452.

Long, S. A., Winograd, P. A., & Bridge, C. A. (1989). The effects of reader and text characteristics on reports of imagery during and after reading. *Reading Research Quarterly, 24*(3), 353–372.

McGregor, D. (2012). Dramatizing science learning: Findings from a pilot study to re-invigorate elementary science pedagogy for five to seven year olds. *International Journal of Science Education, 34*(8), 1145–1165. doi:10.1080/09 500693.2012.660751

McKean, B., & Sudol, P. (2002). Drama and language arts: Will drama improve student writing? *Youth Theatre Journal, 16*(1), 28–37.

Merleau-Ponty, M. (1968). *The visible and the invisible.* Evanston, IL: Northwestern University Press.

O'Neill, C. (1995). *Drama worlds.* Portsmouth, NH: Heinemann.

Pohlman, C. (2008). *Revealing minds: Assessing to understand and support struggling readers.* San Francisco, CA: Wiley.

Rosenblatt, L. (1978). *The reader, the text, the poem.* Carbondale, IL: Southern Illinois University Press.

Sadoski, M. (2009). Embodied cognition, discourse, and dual coding theory. In J. Renkema (Ed.), *Discourse, of course: An overview of research in discourse studies* (pp. 187–195). Amsterdam/Philadelphia: John Benjamins Publishing Company.

Shanahan, M.-C., & Nieswandt, M. (2009). Creative activities and their influence on identification in science: Three case studies. *Journal of Elementary Science Education, 21*(3), 63–79.

Tortello, R. (2004). Tableaux vivants in the literature classroom. *The Reading Teacher, 58*(2), 206–208.

Varelas, M., Pappas, C. P., Tucker-Raymond, E., Kane, J., Hankes, J., Ortiz, I., & Keblawe-Shamah, N. (2010). Drama activities as ideational resources for primary-grade children in urban science classrooms. *Journal of Research in Science Teaching, 47*(3), 302–305. doi:10.1002/tea.20336

Vygotsky, L. S. (2004). Imagination and creativity in childhood. *Journal of Russian and East European Psychology, 42*(1), 7–97. Retrieved from: www.marxists.org/archive/vygotsky/works/imagination.pdf

Vygotsky, L. S. (1978). *Mind in society*. Cambridge, MA: Harvard University Press.

Wilson, G. P. (2003). Supporting young children's thinking through tableau. *Language Arts 80*(5), 375–383.

4 Learning through group process

Having discussed the impact of tableau on reading behaviour and cognition, this chapter examines the learning to be gained from the *collective* experience of composing tableau. The chapter begins by exploring the human experience of being 'one among many' alongside the philosophies of Jean-Luc Nancy and Maurice Merleau-Ponty. This is followed by a description of a recent study that found social integration to be a vital contributing factor for longevity of life. Returning to the classroom study at the heart of this book, I draw on Gallagher and Ntelioglou's observation, "Drama thrives, *however imperfectly*, on the idea that a diverse group of people can come together and make meaning" (2011, p. 322, italics added) to frame the 'imperfections' of the group work as the dynamics that expanded the students' capacity to learn as individuals within a social context. I conclude the chapter by considering the role of tableau in teacher education. Tableau is presented as a medium for reflection, a tool for imagining improved teaching and learning outcomes and an approach to examining private conflicts that impact the public nature of teaching. The role of transformation is pivotal in each example and tableau is positioned as a *co-constructed* art form that 'unlocks' difficult teaching experiences by identifying the problem and thereby opening the possibility of a solution.

The plurality of being

Jean-Luc Nancy reminds us of the intrinsic connection between human beings when he writes, "The plurality of beings is at the foundation of Being" (2000, p. 12). For Nancy, our sense of who we are as a human being can only exist in relation to other human beings and therefore the concept of existing as a singular human being is a contradiction in terms. As an alternative, Nancy offers three words that define our existential experience – 'being singular plural'. Collectively, these words denote both equality and interdependence, "none of these three terms precedes or grounds the other, each designates the coessence of the others" (p. 37) and none of the terms negate the others, i.e. being part of a plural existence does not negate the experience of being singular, we live all three terms simultaneously. Imprints of this philosophy can be found in Maurice Merleau-Ponty's description of the individual as both "a dimension and a universal" (1968, p. 142). Writing earlier than Nancy, he developed a thesis of human existence as fundamentally co-existence through the reversible flow of connectivity between humans. Selecting the word 'chiasm' as a metaphor for the intertwining experience of existing as a human being among other human beings, Merleau-Ponty evidences co-existence in the mutuality of the perceptive process. We are seen by those we observe, "the seeing is not without visible existence" and when we shake hands "the touched takes hold of the touching" (1968, p. 143). However, this does not mean that one element of the perceptive process subsumes the other, each retains its individual characteristics but both are needed for perception to be experienced.

These philosophies of co-existence have direct application in light of a recent study about longevity of life (Pinker, 2017). Pinker begins her TED talk by describing the lifestyle of the inhabitants on the Mediterranean island of Sardinia, "the only place where men live as long as women" (00:27). She details the village of Villagrande as a place with social cohesion in its architectural fabric of tightly packed houses and crisscrossing alleyways. It is a place where people are always surrounded by family members, friends or community figures and "never left to live solitary lives" (04:13). The description sets the context for a study that involved tens of thousands of people and explored the factors most likely to promote a long life. More than eating healthily and keeping fit, the data evidenced 'social integration' to be the strongest predictor for a life well lived and 'long lived'. Pinker characterised 'social integration' as operating through multiple modes of human expression, "simply making eye contact with somebody, shaking hands, giving somebody a high-five is enough to release oxytocin, which increases your level of trust and it lowers your cortisol levels. So it lowers your stress" (09:51). In essence, these are gestures of connectivity that remind us we are not alone in our existence as a human being.

However, despite the positive outcomes of the study reported above, being among and with others is not always a comfortable experience. Although we share our humanity, we *live* the world from a singular experience, or as Anderson writes, it is our differences we have in common (2016, p. 25). Greene conveys the same sentiment this way, "Even though we are on a common ground, we have different locations on that ground" (1995, p. 156). In the context of how we live our lives, having 'different locations' means we each have our own way of doing things. Biesta frames this reality as both problematic and educational. Firstly, it is problematic in the conundrum it presents – what happens when the capacity for living 'my' life is constrained by limitations in the form of other people wanting to live 'their' life? (2018). And secondly, this conundrum presents a fundamentally educational opportunity for learning how to share a planet that "only has limited capacity for fulfilling our desires" (Biesta, 2018, p. 18). In attempting to address the dilemma of self-expression, agency and finite space and resources, Biesta suggests we develop a heightened sense of ourselves as 'subjects'. This may sound counter-intuitive until we read his definition of subject,

> To exist as subject does not mean to simply escape from any external determination, but to ponder the question of limits and limitations, the questions of when, how and to what extent we should limit and transform our own desires in the face of the desires of others and in the face of an environment – a planet – that just isn't able to give us everything we want.
>
> (2018, pp. 14–15)

He describes this way of existing as a 'grown-up' way – realising the necessity of living in 'dialogue' with others without "occupying the centre of the world" (p. 15). According to Biesta, we become 'grown up' through being around others and holding our subject-ness in tension as we choose whether to persist with our intentions, negotiate our intentions or refrain from our intentions – all in the process of dialogue. Putting 'grown-up-ness' into practice is neither about exerting self-will nor capitulating to others but rather acting out of an awareness that leaves space for others to exist as subjects as well. In this way, the 'space' becomes an educational opportunity for teaching us about our interdependence, "namely that *you are not alone*" (Biesta, p. 16, italics in the original). Process drama could be considered a unique educational opportunity for realising and practicing our interdependence. Heathcote claims, "Dramatic work is first and foremost a social art" (1984, p. 196) and Schneider, Crumpler and Rogers agree, "Process drama is primarily social because it is realised in the company of others and involves negotiation and renegotiation of meaning as participants interpret and reinterpret their own views in concert with participants in a drama sequence" (2006, p. xiv). As we shall see, the processes of creating through negotiation presented challenges for the third grade (Year 4) students and a part of this constraint grew from individual recognition of a "growing responsibility to the group's effort" (O'Neill in Schneider, Crumpler & Rogers, 2006, p. xi). According to Biesta, such an awareness would signify learning to exist in a 'grown-up' way.

Constraints in the arts

Biesta's theory is relevant in this current discourse because as suggested above, he positions the arts as presenting unique opportunities for developing a grown-up subjectivity through 'resistances' encountered in the creative process. First of all, Biesta points to the resistance encountered in the material of an art form itself, be it paint, wood, sound or our own body. Each medium presents limits that need to be worked *with* in order to create meaning. De Vos views dance as enhancing Biesta's formulation of subjectivity because dancers' bodies are connected, and therefore somewhat constricted, to each other in motion, "To talk less and to do more, to feel and experience more together. The development of mind and body, of one's subjectivity and intersubjectivity, should go hand in hand" (2018, p. 69).

To suggest one's subjectivity is developed through co-expression and constriction inverts the idea of the arts being a means for channelling self-expression. Bolton, writing in opposition to this populist view, states that drama "is not about self-expression; it is a form of group symbolism seeking universal, not individual truths" (1985, p. 154). Process drama conventions such as tableau are contingent on participants interacting with each other in order to make meaning. Nevertheless, tensions become visible when group members attempt to 'exist in dialogue' during a creative process while negotiating opposing viewpoints, temperaments and styles of working. And yet in Biesta's framework, it is these very resistances, resulting from each human being working alongside other human beings, that form the conditions necessary for learning *how* to 'exist in dialogue' with others.

Constraints in the classroom study

In light of the discussion above, I want to focus on the classroom study and examine the inherent constraints imposed by the design of the study and the struggles of the students to 'exist in dialogue' with each other. Findings about group process are based on audio transcripts, video, time-lapse images and student written responses.

Group process

When students were asked what they liked about drama class in a 2014 Canadian report, one student answered she appreciated the opportunity to make "friends with people you thought you'd never be friends with" (McLauchlan & Winters, p. 58). Having experienced this in my own classroom teaching, I made the decision prior to meeting the students to randomly assign them into five groups. Student views about working in groups they had been assigned to emerged when they wrote in response to a series of questions about the study experience. When asked what they did not enjoy about the study, three replies were about other group members (they did not name them) and one reply stated, "My group, not saying I did not like the kids, just that it would be better if I was with my BFF". If I had been able to interview this student further, I would have been interested to know in what sense they used the word "better". Groups did not always work well together and throughout the study there was a particular group that experienced problems with the collaborative nature of the work. They often argued about the mechanics of tasks such as the reading of text or the writing of the main idea sentence and this sometimes resulted in group members carrying out disparate activities. As I looked at video data of them 'working together', I saw that their assigned place (by me) had been in the far corner of the room, furthest away from the space where the tableaux were shared at the end of the session. They were in a very small area of the classroom and behind them was a table covered with assorted back-packs, lunch bags and coats. These observations caused me to wonder about the impact of the environment on working patterns and if my decision to put them in a cluttered, crowded space had affected their ability to engage as a group. Nevertheless, the time-lapse images from the sessions recorded how each group was able to ultimately work with environmental resistances of noise and space (five groups in one classroom) to prepare and finally present a tableau of a main idea to the rest of the class. The shared purpose of creating tableau caused a 'centering' of activity (Branscombe & Schneider, 2018); individual actions when trialling different gestures and positions were energetically orchestrated alongside students adjusting the positioning of other group members and swapping roles with each other (see Chapter 3).

Group process through talk

Douglas Barnes (2008) believes teachers need to give greater considera-
tion to the types of talk they make possible in their classrooms. He coun-
sels that the way teachers organise communication in the classroom will
affect the how and what of student learning. When introducing new ideas,
he advocates a constructivist approach prioritising 'exploratory talk', which
he characterises as "hesitant and incomplete because it enables the speaker
to try out ideas, to hear how they sound, to see what others make of them,
to arrange information and ideas into different patterns" (p. 5). This notion
of ideas being re-formed as they are spoken aloud accords with Vygotsky's
theory that speaking shapes thought and this is enhanced when developing
ideas alongside others (1978). Darlington makes the additional point that
being exposed to other's thoughts can 'widen and deepen' an individual's
understanding of topics (2010).

Exploratory talk was certainly a feature of student talk in the classroom
study. Digital recorders were placed in the middle of each group and switched
on as soon as the students assembled to discuss the text and the main idea.
Recorders stayed on throughout the discussion of text and the devising of
tableau. The collection of data through audio recordings became an important data source for tracking intra-group communication about the creative
process. The discourse resulting from student interactions was intended to
provide an insider's perspective, i.e. that of the students, on the processes of
representing main ideas as they prepared their tableaux. I did not intervene
in their discussions unless they asked a question. I made the methodological
decision to not 'interrogate' the students about their creative choices and to
not ask them why they represented main ideas in certain ways in case the
very act of questioning changed their decisions. As Daniel Walsh writes,
"[Children] have come to expect that when adults ask them questions, either
the adult already knows the answer ... or they are in trouble" (Graue &
Walsh, 1998, p. 113). I hoped that any "why" questions I had about group
process might be answered in the recordings of their discussions.

Mercer reminds us that as social beings we "gain much of what we know
from others" (2002, p. 153) and in the process of composing a tableau based
on a key concept, students were exposed to the ideas of others. They built
upon and adjusted each other's imaginings in "a multi-voiced process of
debate, negotiation and orchestration" (Engeström & Sannino, 2010, p. 5).
The following transcript records how members of one group composed their

tableau about a solar eclipse through a collective network of verbal suggestions and physical demonstrations:

Student 1:	You go here and then ...
Student 2:	You go like this and then like that.
Student 3:	You both, I'm going to be behind you.
Student 1:	Ok, put your feet here.
Student 2:	I'm the sun and then me and Owen face each other.
Student 1:	Yea!
Student 4:	I'm gonna be like this.
Student 1:	Yea, you go like that and then ...
Student 3:	Yea, that's an awesome idea!

In this positive example of 'existing in dialogue', we can read how the shared purpose of tableau elicited a focus on *individual* poses by *everyone* in the group. As *co-authors* of the tableau, they praised and affirmed each other's creative choices for embodying aspects of a solar eclipse and valued the contribution of each performative gesture.

It is tempting to critique students who were vocally dominant as being resistant to the idea of dialogue. That said, a closer scrutiny of their verbal contributions (to initiate the rereading of text, express an opinion on what they believed was the main idea or claim a role) revealed that their talk often provoked discussion and helped to maintain purpose and group focus on the task. Regarding role, Wagner states that "participants in drama must negotiate their roles. Unless they agree and cooperate the game is over" (1998, p. 28). However, video and audio data captured the difficulty many groups had in agreeing on roles. Roles were generally claimed, sometimes assigned and less often negotiated. The following transcript evidences a fairly typical exchange between two students in conflict over role group,

Student 1:	I'll be the moon.
Student 2:	No. I want to be the moon.
Student 1:	I'm the moon.
Student 2:	You're Earth.
Student 1:	No, can I be the moon?
Student 2:	I'm the moon.
Student 1:	Ok, I'll be Earth.

While it appears that student 2 deployed their agency more successfully than student 1, it could be argued that student 1 was negotiating rather than capitulating and therefore manifesting a grown-up-ness as defined by Biesta previously. The student 'refrained' from persisting with their desire to be the moon because they prioritised the task of composing a tableau above their individual need to role-play the moon. This student agreed to an alternative role and thereby made room for the other student's persistence to be fulfilled. However, I am aware that this example could be viewed negatively as evidence of 'browbeating' and indeed one of the most troubling aspects of group work is when individual students appear to deny space for alternative viewpoints. Having witnessed this occurring at times during the classroom study, I had the students write in response to the following question: What did your group do when it couldn't agree on the main idea? One disgruntled student wrote, "Kathryn (a pseudonym) told us what to do, but the last time I took a stand and refused". Whilst acknowledging this as one student's version of what happened in their group, it does suggest a summoning of agency in order to confront a group member who in their opinion was not making space for other viewpoints (Tudge & Hogan, 2005).

More 'positive' responses revealed a variety of strategies to overcome instances of resistance during the creative process. These included solving a conflict through discussion, referring back to the text, voting on an idea or abandoning an idea that was causing conflict. I believe these opportunities to meet conflict and negotiate differences helped the students develop a grown-up-ness as defined earlier by Biesta. The task of creating a group representation of a main idea gave focus to human interactions, and helped students persevere in the face of interactions they perceived as resistances to group process.

The constraints of tableau

In the classroom study, certain constraints originated with the informational texts themselves. They were texts designed for efferent reading (Rosenblatt, 1978), i.e. they communicated knowledge for the students to take away in order to learn about the solar system. The texts were not poetic or particularly descriptive or full of emotive language and yet the students were asked to create artistic structures in response to them. People roles were introduced in tableaux when no reference had been made to humans within the information texts but this constraint did not inhibit the students from finding a role for them within their tableaux. As we saw from detailed analysis in Chapter 3, the students worked with those constraints and *collaboratively* produced tableau infused with traditionally fictional devices of emotion and narrative. In the creative process, students offered different perspectives on how they could bring these texts 'to life'. Here is an extract from one group discussing their tableau based on Text 6. It reveals that while two students are claiming 'dead' or 'dying' roles to show what a sunless planet would be like, the other students in the group introduce some levity with a narrative involving animals chasing each other,

Student 1:   I want to be a polar bear dying.
Student 2:   I was going to be a dead person.
Student 1:   Yea, you can be a dead person.
Student 3:   I could be this little bird.
Student 4:   I'm gonna be a chipmunk. I could be chasing you.
Student 3:   Oh yea, that's good, that's good.

Another potential constraint related to the texts was that for each session the groups were given the same text. Working in close proximity to each other could have resulted in similar representations of main ideas. Yet this did not happen once. Figure 4.1 is one group's representation of the gravitational pull between the sun and the Earth. It is a comedic scene of an Earth desperate to escape the gravitational force of the sun but unable to do. Other groups portrayed this same concept quite differently; one group had two students in role as gravity, standing either side of the sun and towering with arms outstretched above a cowering Earth and another group had the sun holding aloft the foot of gravity who managed to balance on the other leg while firmly holding a submissive Earth in place.

The final constraint to be considered in this discussion of the classroom study is that of tableau as a motionless structure. This 'brevity' of form brings challenges to those who create tableau. Many of the informational texts were about concepts to do with movement of the planetary objects or the emission of a force or energy source and this meant students had to carefully consider how they would show motion through stillness. They did this by expansive stances and extended limbs to depict transfer and activity. In Figure 4.1, we see a tableau bursting with movement *through still poses* and as we gaze at the image, we feel the *force* from the sun, the *pull* of gravity and the desperate *effort* on the part of the Earth to get away – all effectively

Figure 4.1 Students show movement through still poses.

conveyed through stillness. It might have been 'easier' and funnier to have shown Earth actually running on the spot while gravity kept stretching forward but it would not have captured the dynamic interplay of the relationship between the roles. The control needed to show movement through held poses requires a concentrated attention to every detail of stance, gesture and facial expression. Diderot, as cited in Barthes, describes a well-composed tableau as a "whole contained under a single point of view, in which the parts work together to one end and form by their mutual correspondence a unity" (1977, p. 71) and I believe that for the most part, the tableaux achieved that unity of form and function to represent main ideas.

Tableau in teacher education

The chapter concludes with descriptions of how tableau has been used in three different teacher education contexts. The research accounts are based on studies that investigated tableau as an instrument for reflecting on teaching experiences and a tool for imagining future classroom practice. Both studies were conducted in partnership with my dissertation supervisor at the University of South Florida, Dr Jenifer Jasinski Schneider. The third account features the recollection of a teacher educator who attended a literacy conference and experienced personally the transformative potential of tableau.

Study one

In many teacher education programmes, the dominant mode for reflecting on teaching practice is through written documentation. As teacher educators, our concern was that these "text-based literacy practices mediate reflection in particular, text-based ways" (Branscombe & Schneider, 2013, p. 48) and did not sufficiently capture the 'messiness' and confusion of classroom life. We felt drawn towards Boud's view of reflection as involving "the unprocessed, raw material of experience and engaging with it as a way to make sense of what has occurred" (2001, p. 10) and Schön's theory of reflection-in-action as particularly suited to "situations of uncertainty or uniqueness" (1983, p. 69), for example, classrooms. Schön defines someone who reflects-in-action as "a researcher in the practice context … [who] does not keep means and ends separate, but defines them interactively as he [sic] frames a problematic situation" (p. 68). Although Schön was not referring to tableau when he wrote those words, the references to 'interactive definitions' and the 'framing of problematic situations' are perfectly suited to the practice of activism through tableau.

In designing a study based on active reflection, we were also influenced by the precepts within Augusto Boal's Theatre of the Oppressed manifesto (1979) and his practice of Image Theatre (1995) as an activist artform. Boal positions theatre as a tool for reflecting back at society oppressive societal structures in order for the locus of oppression to be identified, challenged and transformed. Establishing drama as a means for society to look back at itself, "Theatre is born when the human being discovers it can observe itself; when it discovers that, in this act of seeing, it can see *itself* – see itself *in situ*: see itself seeing" (Boal, 1995, p. 13, italics in the original) invokes comparisons with Merleau-Ponty's discourse on perception as a reciprocal act, the "reversibility of the seeing and the visible" (1968, p. 154). Alongside having the student teachers *seeing themselves* engaged in problematic teaching situations from the 'past', we wanted to introduce the notion that reflecting is about looking forward as much as it is looking backwards. With that said, we recognised the potential for tableau to be a 'reflection in action' by enabling student teachers to observe themselves in difficult classroom situations with a view to transforming them in practice.

Method

In a class about integrating the arts into the curriculum, student teachers were asked to bring a written reflection about a troubling classroom moment they had been involved with or had witnessed in their placement school. They were asked to draw a representation of the troubling situation and to label the drawing with a caption. Working in groups, the student teachers shared their drawings with each other. Due to time constraints, they were asked to focus on one particular situation and to create a tableau based on the significant event.

Tableau participants used facial expressions, gestures and spatial positioning to replicate the drawing and as each group presented their tableau, the rest of the class was invited to walk around and through the tableau, 'reading' the embodied components and offering ideas about what was happening in the tableau. They analysed individual gestures, expressions and positions as elements that may have contributed to the difficult situation. For example, one tableau chronicled the moment a student teacher was being observed by her university supervisor as she struggled to review a concept from the previous week. The other tableau members took on the role of the confused students and embodied their firm resistance to all efforts of clarification with angled heads, puzzled expressions and crossed legs. The student teacher's still pose captured the moment of intense frustration and embarrassment through raised shoulders, an exasperated outstretched palm, wide eyes and tightly closed lips. In analysing these gestures, it was suggested that they may have provoked the growing resentment of the class and therefore shut down their willingness to listen and comprehend.

Borrowing from Augusto Boal's 'Image of Transition' activity (1995, p. 115), each group was then asked to revise their tableau image and create an 'ideal' version of the challenging moment. When these second tableaux were shown, the same process of 'close reading' prevailed – by first of all attending to the overall message of the image and then isolating contrasting elements of gesture, expression and social distances between the characters in the tableau. The student teachers observed how supportive teaching stances were conveyed through smiles, relaxed hand gestures and positioning that conveyed an intention to help rather than remain distant – for example, when giving individual help, bending down towards the pupil rather than standing over them. These observations were based on the precept that transformation is possible, not just ideal, if we attend to the embodied components that were analysed in the tableaux – gesture, expression and positioning. For Boal, the juxtaposition of the 'real' event alongside the 'ideal' situation provokes the key question that leads to transformation – "how may it be possible to go from the first [image] to the second" (1995, p. 115)?

Asking student teachers to discuss 'how do we get from tableau A to tableau B in our classrooms' provoked the sharing of practical instructional strategies and heightened awareness of gesture and expression as affective factors in generating positive and negative teaching and learning outcomes. "In frozen moments, the student teachers became different characters and attended to the message of their gestures and understood how their bodies sent important instructional signals to their students" (Branscombe & Schneider, 2018, p. 33).

Empathy

In writing about empathy as a defining quality of the human species, Vittorio Gallese posits that "the capacity for understanding others as intentional agents is deeply grounded in the relational nature of action. Action is relational, and the relation holds both between the agent and the object target of the action" (2001, p. 33). Participating in these reflection tableaux appeared to amplify the relational dynamic of action between agents (teachers) and the object targets of the action (pupils). As a result, student teachers changed their perspectives about troubled students in their classroom placements and became more empathetic towards them. This was particularly the case when individual participants in tableaux were invited to remain in role but to 'step-out' of the tableau and voice aloud a thought their character role might be having at that troublesome moment. In one tableau, a pupil had a temper tantrum while waiting in line to have work marked. The teacher and the other pupils ignored the pupil, suggesting this was a regular occurrence. The student teacher in role as the pupil revealed that her "extended time on the floor, with arm outstretched towards the teacher, helped her understand what the child might be feeling. She physically felt the rejection of the teacher and the dismissive/curious stares of the classmates" (Branscombe & Schneider, 2013, p. 59). When the frustrated pupil was given a chance to 'step out' of the tableau and voice their thoughts, the comments revealed social isolation and a lack of understanding of the work. In response to this, the second image was re-sculpted to depict a teacher engaged in proactive instruction that helped the pupil be successful in their work. As a result of witnessing this tableau, one student teacher remarked,

> Often when we reflect, we think about what happened and what we can do to fix it, and not why it is happening in the first place. Thinking

for the character in the reflection aids in determining the trigger for the situation.

These words allude to an increase in empathy borne out of seeing the problematic situation from the perspective of the one who was supposedly the *cause* of the problem. On hearing the words of the 'problem pupil' speaking from 'inside' the tableau, the viewer becomes intertwined with their perspective and we are reminded once again of Merleau-Ponty's formulation of perception as a reversible process.

Collaborative witnessing

A surprising outcome of the study, and one that links back to the beginning of the chapter, was the shared sense of relief among the student teachers that they were not alone in experiencing problematic teaching situations. In contrast to traditional written reflections shared privately between a student teacher and their supervisor, the public presentation of tableaux became an act of 'collaborative witnessing' (Ellis & Rawicki, 2013) to the fact that all was not necessarily well in their field placements. Although based on individual experiences, there were commonalities of themes between tableaux that depicted classrooms with 'problem' students and/or frustrated teachers. The singular experiences student teachers had witnessed and represented in tableaux became universal problems for us all to solve. The 'solving' of these problems through a revised tableau presented an opportunity to work out how the different 'subjects' in classroom life can put into practice Biesta's philosophy of 'existing in dialogue' with each other. Crucially, these non-verbocentric reflections on specific teaching moments afforded the public representation of present realities *and* future possibilities.

Study two

Conducted as part of a writing methods course, this study reoriented our focus towards the study of tableau as a vessel for student teachers to imagine future teaching acts and thereby provide teacher educators with information about student teachers' developing pedagogical theories (Branscombe & Schneider, 2018). As with the first study described above, we remained unconvinced "that writing about teaching actually creates the pedagogical change teacher educators want to see in classrooms. Rather, we want[ed] candidates to become better in the act of teaching by actually seeing and embodying the possibilities for pedagogical change" (p. 20).

Context

The study occurred during a six-day field placement at a private school. The school provided iPads for all of its students and in contrast to the state schools had welcomed the idea of the research project. The purpose of the field placement was to teach student teachers how to work alongside pupils in the production of written and digital media. The student teachers attended seminars before and after each school day where they were exposed to instructional strategies that would support them as they worked with the Year 5 pupils. During one of these sessions the student teachers were asked to work in groups and create a tableau of an unproductive writing session that they had experienced themselves when they were at school or during a previous school placement. Framing this scene as a 'problem' that needed transforming, we again applied Boal's "image of transition" technique and asked the student teachers to compose an alternative tableau of an ideal classroom where writing was fostered and not stifled. We took photographs of the contrasting tableaux and used these as data for analysing differences in staging, character, social distance and gesture between the tableau representations.

Observations

Tableau depictions of unproductive writing classrooms showed isolated students seemingly disconnected from other bodies in the classroom. In contrast, the 'ideal' classrooms featured circular patterns of bodies where teachers worked shoulder to shoulder with students or sat on a rug to be at the same level with their students rather than placing themselves at a distance and in opposition to their students. We also noticed marked differences in gesture between the first and second tableau. In the ideal images, the gestures of the teacher roles denoted the encouragement rather than chastisement of students. Hands became a focal point for observation because they were used in such contrasting ways between the before and after tableau,

> When we specifically examined hand gestures, we identified the orientation of hands as most indicative of intentional teaching. The hands

communicated, through a relaxed yet energetic outstretched stance, that student responses were encouraged. Conversely, hands conveyed disapproval if they were used to point or if hands were positioned in a downward orientation, such as when placed on the hips.

(p. 32)

What we learned

These transformed tableau were based on the student teachers' imagined representations of how they saw themselves in the future as teachers who could stimulate productive writing spaces. In addition, the opportunity to re-sculpt problematic teaching spaces "allowed them to visualise solutions and take action with everyone's best interest in mind" (p. 34). And as teacher educators, these depictions "gave us an opportunity to observe these changing insights" (p. 35). Above all, these tableau representations placed imagination as an instructional tool for teacher education and facilitated an acknowledgement of past events as an opportunity to change the future.

Transforming private fears

The examples above show how sharing experience and imagined futures through embodied representations can be a means to a transformative outcome. The tableaux shared by the student teachers were the embodied tracings of their developing identities as professional teachers. What follows is an example of using tableau to unlock a personal conflict between a private and professional identity. As previously noted, process drama conventions such as tableau may be based on personal experiences, but they are not conduits for self-expression and as we shall see, the sharing of a personal story through tableau yielded consequences that extended beyond the private experience and into the public space that is teaching.

A few years ago, I led a workshop at a literacy conference on the theme of 'tableau for transformation'. After describing how I had used tableau as a reflective tool with student teachers, I asked participants to form groups and within those groups to each share a difficult teaching or learning experience which could become the focus for Boal's 'Image of Transition' approach to tableau (see earlier). A doctoral student who was also a teacher educator shared a personal story that became the basis for a tableau representation. What follows is her recollection of the transformative potential of tableau,

There have been events at my university that I wanted my children to experience. My preservice teachers could be at these events and I struggled with whether to bring my youngest son. He is a special needs child, which can lead to disruptive behaviour when he becomes unregulated. As a teacher educator, I often focus on classroom management and behaviour. What would my preservice teachers think if I was at an event with them and my son was disruptive? Would it undermine my credibility with them? The tableau we created was focused on my concern – I was with my son, who is being disruptive, at a university event. Off to the side are some of my preservice teachers, who are talking behind their hands as they discuss my credibility as a teacher educator.

The experience of talking through how to design the tableau and my positioning within the tableau illuminated how strongly I felt about this fear. I didn't realize the emotional connection I had to this concern until it was manifested into the tableau. Upon reflection, I realized that my son's challenges should be used as a teaching opportunity with my students, rather than positioning myself (and him) within a deficit perspective.

For this PhD student, tableau was the key to unlocking an embedded and private fear and transforming it into an opportunity to teach *others* through a very *personal* reality. Of equal significance, when she shared her story with her group, they felt something had been unlocked in them too. Her honesty and willingness to be vulnerable strengthened their resolve to support her as she strove to balance the pressures of family and academic life. What she had considered as a personal narrative of 'shame' became an opportunity for confronting false concepts of credibility and professionalism. The personal dilemma ceased being a problem to be hidden away *from* the students she taught and instead became a teaching opportunity to share *with* her students.

Summary

The body is a thing that can be alienated from the mind and the heart; when we pull them together and make simple gestures as a group, I believe that there is something that is unlocked. The Ancient Greeks knew it, people have known it in all sorts of traditional societies, there is something that gives us strength there.

(Bill T. Jones – choreographer, 2001)

According to Smagorinsky, "The kind of psychology that's practiced in schools is concerned with and almost exclusively focused on the mind of the individual student" (2014). This reductive psychology alongside an increasingly academic curriculum has led to a fevered competitiveness between students, schools, regions and even countries in the form of Programme for International Student Assessment (PISA) rankings. The nature of embodied learning as a group representation of understanding offers an alternative focus away from 'the mind of the individual student' and interrupts the endless cycle of individual striving. The exposure to others' perspectives, experiences, dispositions and desires strengthens our plurality as human beings, even when the experience is difficult. Group work develops our 'grown-up-ness' as described by Biesta earlier and our understanding of alternative realities as experienced by others (Greene, 1995). The realisation that others think and do differently 'unlocks' a fixation on individual experience and leads to strengthened bonds between people. Presenting opportunities to work together and to use our bodies in working together deepens our connection and identity as human beings who need each other.

References

Anderson, A. W. (2016). "Out of everywhere into here": Rhetoricity and transcendence as common ground for spiritual research. In J. Lin, R. L. Oxford & T. Culham (Eds.), *Towards a spiritual research paradigm: Exploring new ways of knowing, researching and being* (pp. 25–53). Charlotte, NC: Information Age Publishing Inc.

Barnes, D. R. (2008). Exploratory talk for learning. In N. Mercer & S. Hodgkinson (Eds.), *Exploring talk in schools* (pp. 1–15). Los Angeles, CA: Sage.

Barthes, R. (1977). *Image music text*. New York: Hill and Wang.

Biesta, G. (2018). What if: Art education beyond expression and creativity. In C. Naughton, G. Biesta & D. R. Cole (Eds.), *Arts, artists and pedagogy: Philosophy and the arts in education* (pp. 11–20). London and New York: Routledge.

Boal, A. (1995). *The rainbow of desire*. London: Routledge.

Boal, A. (1979). *Theatre of the oppressed*. London: Pluto Press.

Bolton, G. (1985). Changes in thinking about drama in education. *Theory into Practice, 24*(3), 151–157.

Boud, D. (2001). Using journal writing to enhance reflective practice. *New Directions for Adult and Continuing Education, 90*, 9–17.

Branscombe, M., & Schneider, J. J. (2018). Accessing teacher candidates' pedagogical intentions and imagined teaching futures through drama and arts-based structures. *Action in Teacher Education, 40*(1), 19–37.

Branscombe, M., & Schneider, J. J. (2013). Embodied discourse: Using tableau to explore preservice teachers' reflections and activist stances. *Journal of Language and Literacy Education*, *9*(1), 48–65. Retrieved from: http://jolle.coe.uga.edu/volume-91-2013/

Darlington, H. (2010). Teaching secondary school science through drama. *School Science Review*, *91*(337), 109–113.

De Vos, N. (2018). Bodily connectedness in motion: A philosophy in intercorporeity and the art of dance in education. In C. Naughton, G. Biesta & D. R. Cole (Eds.), *Arts, artists and pedagogy: Philosophy and the arts in education* (pp. 61–70). London and New York: Routledge

Ellis, C., & Rawicki, J. (2013). Collaborative witnessing of survival during the Holocaust: An exemplar of relational autoethnography. *Qualitative Inquiry*, *19*(4), 366–380.

Engeström, Y., & Sannino, A. (2010). Studies of expansive learning: Foundations, findings and future challenges. *Educational Research Review*, *5*(1), 1–24.

Gallagher, K., & Ntelioglou, B. Y. (2011). Which new literacies? Dialogue and performance in youth writing. *Journal of Adolescent and Adult Literacy*, *54*(5), 322–330.

Gallese, V. (2001). The 'shared manifold' hypothesis: From mirror neurons to empathy. *Journal of Consciousness Studies*, *8*(5–7), 33–50.

Graue, M. E., & Walsh, D. J. (1998). *Studying children in context: Theories, methods, and ethics*. Thousand Oaks, CA: Sage.

Greene, M. (1995). Releasing the imagination: Essays on education, the arts, and social change. San Francisco, CA: Jossey-Bass.

Heathcote, D. (1984). The authentic teacher and the future. In L. Johnson, & C. O'Neill, (Eds.), *Collected writings on education and drama*. Evanston, IL: Northwestern University Press.

Jones, B. T. (2001, September 19). The 11th of September (B. Moyers, interviewer) [Video file]. Retrieved from: www.pbs.org/moyers/journal/archives/billtjones_911_flash.html

McLauchlan, D., & Winters, K. (2014). What's so great about drama class? Year 1 secondary students have their say. *Research in Drama Education: The Journal of Applied Theatre and Performance*, *19*(1), 51–63.

Mercer, N. (2002). Developing dialogues. In G. Wells & G. Claxton (Eds.), *Learning for life in the 21st century: Sociocultural perspectives on the future of education* (pp. 141–153). Oxford, United Kingdom: Blackwell.

Merleau-Ponty, M. (1968). *The visible and the invisible*. Evanston, IL: Northwestern University Press.

Nancy, J.-L. (2000). *Being singular plural*. Stanford, CA: Stanford University Press.

Pinker, S. (2017, April 17). The secret to living longer may be your social life [video]. Retrieved from: www.ted.com/talks/susan_pinker_the_secret_to_living_longer_may_be_your_social_life

Rosenblatt, L. (1978). *The reader, the text, the poem*. Carbondale, IL: Southern Illinois University Press.

Schneider, J. J., Crumpler, T. P., & Rogers, T. (Eds.). (2006). *Process drama and multiple literacies*. Portsmouth, NH: Heinemann.

Schön, D. (1983). *The reflective practitioner*. New York: Basic Books.

Smagorinsky, P. (2014). Why our kids need drama. *Psychology Today*. Retrieved from: www.psychologytoday.com/blog/conceptual-revolution/201401/why-our-kids-need-drama

Tudge, J., & Hogan, D. (2005). An ecological approach to observations of children's everyday lives. In S. Greene & D. Hogan (Eds.), *Researching children's experience: Approaches and methods* (pp. 102–122). Thousand Oaks, CA: Sage.

Vygotsky, L. S. (1978). *Mind in society*. Cambridge, MA: Harvard University Press.

Wagner, B. J. (1998). *Educational drama and language arts: What research shows*. Portsmouth, NH: Heinemann.

5   We all have bodies, don't we?

In this final chapter, findings from the classroom study are summarised, and additional examples of teaching science through embodied learning are presented. As I wrote in the preface, it is my hope that this monograph will inspire teachers to be more intentional about using the body in teaching and learning. The ideas are included to be a spark for readers to use in their own context.

A synthesis of findings

The following synthesis is provided to summarise how students represented main ideas from science information texts as a tableau. The synthesis is divided between the **process of representation** when students discussed the text and practised their ideas for a tableau and the final **tableau representation** presented to the rest of the class.

Process of representation

When discussing the text and practising their tableau ideas, the students represented main ideas from science information texts by:

- Rereading the text
- Using talk to negotiate roles and ideas about the composition of the tableau
- Using exploratory talk to build upon each other's ideas
- Using action to try out different ideas for their tableau
- Referring to the text as the source of information for role and tableau ideas
- Manipulating their own and other bodies into different shapes

- Using different group members in practicing a particular image
- Commenting on the effectiveness of each other's poses and gestures

Final tableau representations

When students presented their tableaux, they represented main ideas from science information texts by:

- Choosing roles that were either directly referenced in the text (the sun, the moon, the Earth), inferred from the text (an ice cream truck in a tableau about the sun's warmth) or not referenced at all but made sense within the context of the text (a student in role as a surprised "OMG human" reacting to a solar eclipse)
- Enacting the text through gesture – using hands, facial expression, posture and positioning in relation to other students. These embodied moves helped students make sense of the text (showing energy forces by stretching out arms and legs) and evidenced their understanding of text (people in shriveled, curled up, isolated positions to show what the absence of the sun would do to life on Earth)
- 'Narrativizing' the main ideas by including people conducting specific actions ("a guy that's trying to shade from the sun") or imbuing roles with emotional content ("a disappointed bird")
- Using gesture to denote emotion (a mother tenderly comforting her dying baby as the sun withdraws its warmth)
- Using different postures to denote main idea roles – height for the sun and lower levels for roles that depend on the sun's power (the Earth, people on Earth)
- Using expansive gestures for the sun to denote its role as the centre of the solar system and sustainer of life on Earth
- Using positioning to denote connectivity between roles (students in the middle position of a tableau depicting gravity as a force between the sun and the Earth) or distance (the intentional space between the car driving to the sun and the sun itself)

So what did the tableau do?

Creating tableau was an engaging and active experience for the students. It gave the third grade students an opportunity to get out from behind their desks, read informational texts purposefully, discuss ideas collaboratively and use their bodies intentionally to represent main ideas. Transforming the informational passages into tableau representations brought about a chiasm of Louise Rosenblatt's efferent and aesthetic reading stances (1978). The students read the texts efferently – as texts communicating scientific principles and aesthetically – as texts that could be interpreted into artefacts of meaning.

In viewing the tableaux created by classmates, students were exposed to *different* ways of representing the same text. This helped not only to promote the role of imagination in the classroom but as *visual texts* the scientific concepts became less abstract and more concrete. Lenters and Winters write, "Current research in the area of literacy and 21st century learning urges elementary educators to expand notions of literacy teaching and learning beyond the focus on reading and writing with paper-based print texts" (2013, p. 227). They describe non-print based texts as "nonlinear texts" and believe that students must gain proficiency in "interpreting" such texts because they are increasingly surrounded by them.

The study expanded what it is to comprehend text by having the students embody a new text based on information in the original text. More than transposing information, the students were *transforming* information across media and showing comprehension in and through their bodies, such as portraying streams of energy from the sun through extended arms and leg gestures that pointed towards the Earth. This comprehension was also evident in writing in role compositions based on the tableau representations. Students wrote about key concepts from an affective perspective, combining elements of narrative with appropriate emotions. These insightful interpretations of how space objects might be feeling during a solar eclipse exemplified Heathcote's affordance of drama as "thinking from within" a situation (1984). The example of a moon revelling in its ability to block out the sun was a well-chosen and humorous sentiment that also revealed the student understood the key concept of what happens during a solar eclipse.

Finally, the creation of tableau was a collaborative activity conducted in a particular classroom context. This dialectical relationship between activity and context was evidenced in the audio and visual data that captured the fluctuations in student focus as they negotiated a combined representation of a main idea. The transcripts revealed struggles to remain in dialogue with each other at times during the creative process. However, the final tableau representations were affirmations of working *with* imperfections to create an embodied and collective response to the informational texts.

Additional examples of embodied learning

The following information describes additional sessions I have delivered to students, teachers and researchers across the country. These sessions have introduced participants to active and embodied techniques for learning about digestion, materials and particle physics.

Digestion

In the English programme of science for Year 4 students, the statutory requirement (a key concept that the students must learn) is for pupils to "describe the simple functions of the basic parts of the digestive system in humans" (Department for Education, 2013, p. 21). The non-statutory requirements are for pupils to "be introduced to the main body parts associated with the digestive system, for example, mouth, tongue, teeth, oesophagus, stomach and small and large intestine and explore questions that help them to understand their special functions" (p. 21). It also suggests pupils might "draw and discuss their ideas about the digestive system and compare them with models or images" (p. 21). When I reviewed these requirements I saw the opportunity for an embodied and immersive experience of learning that involved enacting the different functions of the digestive system. I believed that the embodied representation of the digestive process would be more impressionable than being 'introduced' to the main body parts and looking at disembodied models of the system (Branscombe, 2016/17).

In sessions delivered in schools around the West Midlands, digestion was framed as a 'food journey'. Body parts responsible for the digestive process were named and the children enacted physiological movements as a way of learning about function. For example, they made a swishing action with their hands to show how saliva is a liquid that covers the food in order to break it down and they pushed their hands away from the body to represent the tongue pushing the food into the oesophagus. The stomach was represented by a large group of students encircling a small group of students who stood close together to represent a lump of food. The students in the large circle moved their bodies to mimic the stomach muscles churning the food around. In response, the children in the middle broke apart and ran out of an 'opening' in the stomach.

After leading the students in actions that represented the food journey from ingestion to 'expulsion', the students were invited to work in groups and devise their own set of movements. As students enthusiastically planned their group presentation, they could be heard reviewing the stages of the 'food journey' and naming the main body parts involved. When it was time for groups to show what they had collectively devised, each group's presentation was unique and far more creative than the directed movements I had led them in. The key concepts were embodied through choreographed movements that evolved through the intersection of imagination, collaboration and subject specific knowledge.

Samples of student reflections on the digestion work:

"I enjoyed learning doing actions. I learn't [sic] where your food comes from"

"I enjoyed going through the small intestine"

"What I think was really good was when we all had to put are [sic] hands together and make the oesophagus so that we could let the lumps of food through"

"I enjoyed doing all the different acting and at the end when we did the group work"

"What I enjoyed is when we made up are [sic] own actions in a group. What I learnt is how your body works"

Figure 5.1 shows a student response that speaks of an immersive experience. It references viscerally felt actions ("squishing through"), digestive vocabulary, ("small intestine", "waste"), and acquired knowledge ("I learned that the small intestine was bendy"). I believe the experience of being a lump of food that was 'squished' as it made its way down a "bendy" line of students would lead to greater knowledge retention than examining a three-dimensional model of the digestive system.

Materials

A series of lessons (Branscombe 2017/18) based on the topic 'materials' for Year 5 students used the body to:

- show properties of different materials
- group and compare everyday materials based on their properties
- show why some materials are more suited to certain purposes than others
- show reversible/irreversible changes that occur in different materials

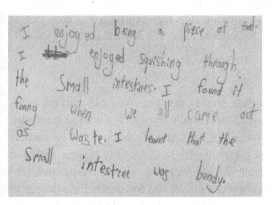

I enjoyed being a piece of food. I enjoyed squishing through the Small intestines. I found it funny when we all came out as Waste. I learnt that the Small intestine was bendy.

Figure 5.1 Student response to embodying the digestive process.

Flashcards with the property descriptors of hard, liquid, strong, tough, magnetic, soft, elastic and waterproof were used as prompts for student-embodied responses. The nature of these properties caused the students to use their bodies in different ways. Some properties were represented by gestures that denoted rigidity (hard, tough, strong), other properties prompted students to move their bodies more fluidly (elastic, liquid) to connect with other students (magnetic) or to 'become' an object with that property (e.g. an umbrella for 'waterproof'). Students were invited to simultaneously 'become' a property from the list and a volunteer student was asked to group similar properties and then explain their choices of groups by referring to similar shapes, gestures and actions that they had identified.

Embodied actions based on concepts of the dissolving process and reversible changes that occur in different materials were based on re-enactments of liquid into ice (reversible) and watching and listening to an effervescent tablet being placed into a glass of water (irreversible). To represent the reversible changes from a liquid into ice and back to a liquid state, students began with fluid actions that became increasingly rigid and then slowly fluid again. For a representation of the dissolving process, the class was split into two groups; one group representing water molecules and the other group the effervescent tablet. The representation began with the water molecule students spinning around the room as a small group of students joined hands to be the tablet and jumped into the middle of the spinning molecules. They then broke apart and also began spinning around to represent the dissolution process and formation of a solution. The representation was engaging to watch and would not have been out of place in a dance class.

Tactile Collider

Tactile Collider is an exciting project that aims to make particle physics accessible to students who are visually impaired (www.tactilecollider. co.uk). Specifically, the workshops delivered in schools focus on particle acceleration and the Large Hadron Collider, the world's biggest and most powerful particle accelerator, 27 kilometres in circumference and constructed beneath the border between France and Switzerland. As the parent of two children who are visually impaired, I was able to attend a workshop and during the session I realised the potential for embodying some of the key concepts through drama. I shared my thoughts with the team of researchers and teachers and a few months later I was invited to deliver a training session on how they might incorporate drama and movement to reinforce the key processes behind particle collision and acceleration.

The Large Hadron Collider (LHC) structure exists to replicate conditions immediately after the universe came into being. Beams of protons are accelerated at 99.999999% to the speed of light in opposite directions and then brought into collision in 4 giant detectors that record the collision and its aftermath. When the two beams collide, the constituents of the protons – quarks – smash together and create new subatomic particles. As I researched these processes, I was struck by the chiasm between abstract concepts and concrete phenomena to describe the creation of matter out of chaotic events. I devised a series of activities that sought to represent those concepts through the use of the body and drama conventions and what follows is a selection of those activities:

1   Key concept – acceleration

This was presented as a 'warm-up' activity that also served to represent the meaning and process of acceleration. Everyone stood in a circle and held hands. I squeezed the hand of the person next to me on my left which then started the 'squeeze' being passed around the circle in a clockwise direction until it came back to me. The next time the squeeze went around the circle it was passed more quickly between participants to represent acceleration. This was done a few times with the aim of speeding up the squeeze each time. Then to represent the collision of protons in the LHC, the squeeze was passed around in both a clockwise and anti-clockwise direction, which meant that someone received a squeeze on their right and left hand simultaneously. This was framed as a moment of collision and was responded to by the person shouting out "collision" and jumping out of the circle very dramatically!

2 Key concept – what happens inside the Large Hadron Collider

The Tactile Collider team participants were asked to work with a partner. Each pair was given one of the statements from the list below and asked to create movements that represented the statements. The statements were:

- Hydrogen atoms are taken from a bottle and stripped of electrons to become protons
- Before entering the LHC the protons are sent through a series of boosters that make them more compact and go faster
- Two beams of protons enter the LHC and travel at 99.99% the speed of light in opposite directions
- When the two beams collide the protons smash into each other and new particles are made from the collision

Each pair demonstrated their choreographed movements, some of which were accompanied by sound effects.

3 Key concept – the moment of collision

A group representation of the moment of collision was dramatised. Six team members were split into two opposing 'bunches' of quarks. The quarks linked themselves closely together and faced the opposing group from opposite ends of the room. On a given signal, the two groups of quarks moved rapidly towards each other and then collided. Photographic data from the LHC has recorded that each time there is a collision, unique patterns of scattering are recorded. Therefore, the collision was repeated several times and in slow motion so that we could experience new shapes being made by bodies in response to each collision event (see Figure 5.2).

Following the activities and with guidance from Robyn Watson, the team member who is also a qualified teacher of the visually impaired, we discussed the application of these activities with students who are visually impaired. The team already had extensive experience delivering Tactile

Figure 5.2 Quarks about to collide.

Collider workshops to students of visual impairment (Dattaro, 2018), and it was felt that the drama activities would reinforce many of the key concepts they teach at present and enhance the workshop opportunities currently offered.

Participant responses

Here is a selection of comments made by the participants in response to the use of drama in teaching particle physics:

"Beyond the impact this will have on TC (Tactile Collider), I can see how this could be applied in many settings".

"The drama 'hands on' exercises were brilliant and got everyone involved, less self conscious and laughing (most importantly). I think the science would also stick much better after it".

"Very useful – I can't lie, I was sceptical at first but there is a lot of potential with these activities".

"It gave me ideas to incorporate science drama into TC, but also into my teaching day job. I think it helped the TC team to be more cohesive as well. It was good to see how we work together with different personality types and how we input".

"Bringing physical drama to reinforce all Tactile activities".

I will finish this section by including the comments made by one of the researchers and project leaders when he was interviewed on the radio.

The observations he makes testify to the cognitive and social gains (see Chapter 4) to be had from working together and using the body in representing scientific concepts.

> So we were a bit nervous being scientists, doing drama for the first time. But we tried it out this week in Scotland and the kids loved it. They joined hands, became a particle accelerator, they acted out what they learned about how dipole magnets bend proton beams, there was lots of laughter, lots of fun. I think it really broke down the barriers and reinforced the science message, so it's been a fantastic success.
>
> (Tactile Collider, 2018)

"I want to be the sun"

"I want to be the sun" was the most frequently spoken intention in the classroom study. It seems fitting therefore to use the sun as a backdrop for my concluding thoughts on what happens when students are able to get out from behind their desks and use their bodies in learning. First of all, the sun is a source for growth. In the classroom study, the students grew through expansive experiences that made space for becoming literate, acquiring knowledge and working alongside others for a creative purpose. Second, the sun gives nourishment as we grow. Students are nourished by exposure to alternative methods for learning and making learning known and this may be particularly the case for the significant number of young people who find a logocentric curriculum hard to digest. Biesta states that what we provide now in schools for our students is a "narrow educational 'diet' – perhaps effective in terms of what can be measured but not very nourishing" (2018, p. 11). As we all know, a narrow diet restricts growth, so if we want our students to grow as learners, we need to expand the diet of what they learn and how they learn. Yes, Sir Ken Robinson, we do all have bodies, so let's use them!

References

Biesta, G. (2018). What if: Art education beyond expression and creativity. In C. Naughton, G. Biesta & D. R. Cole (Eds.), *Arts, artists and pedagogy: Philosophy and the arts in education* (pp. 11–20). London and New York: Routledge.

Branscombe, M. Living in a material world: Using drama to learn about 'materials' in the KS2 science curriculum. *Teaching Drama*, Autumn 1, 2017/18.

Branscombe, M. Digestive drama! Using drama and movement to learn about bones, muscles, nutrition and digestion. *Teaching Drama*, Autumn 1, 2016/17.

Dattaro, L. (2018). LHC exhibit expands beyond the visual. Retrieved from: www.symmetrymagazine.org/article/lhc-exhibit-expands-beyond-the-visual

Department for Education. (2013). National curriculum in England – Science programmes of study: Key stages 1 and 2. Retrieved from: www.gov.uk/government/publications/national-curriculum-in-england-science-programmes-of-study

Heathcote, D. (1984). In L. Johnson & C. O'Neill (Eds.), *Collected writings on education and drama*. Evanston, IL: Northwestern University Press.

Lenters, K. & Winters, K. L. (2013). Fracturing writing spaces. *The Reading Teacher* (*67*)3, 227–237.

Rosenblatt, L. (1978). *The reader, the text, the poem*. Carbondale, IL: Southern Illinois University Press.

Tactile Collider. (2018). Retrieved from: http://tactilecollider.uk/tactile-collider-news.

Index

Page numbers in *italics* refer to figures. Page numbers in **bold** refer to tables.

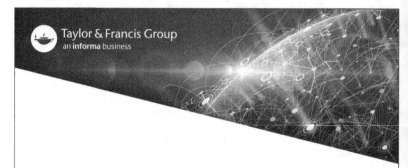

Printed in the United States
by Baker & Taylor Publisher Services